Black Star Over Japan

By the same author

Mongolia
Soul of the Gobi

Black Star Over Japan

RISING FORCES OF MILITARISM

Albert Axelbank

 HILL AND WANG

A division of Farrar, Straus and Giroux

To Koji Nakamura

Writer, editor, and friend, who proposed the title *Black Star Over Japan* to suggest the threat of militarism in his country.

Contents

Preface

Much of this book has grown out of personal experience and research stemming from a dozen years as a writer, journalist, and teacher in Japan. I have interviewed or put questions to many persons, including Socialist Party Chairman Inejiro Asanuma (he was assassinated); author Yukio Mishima (he committed suicide); elder statesman Kenzo Matsumura (he died a natural death); Communist Party Chairman Kenji Miyamoto; Nippon Steel president Yoshitaro Inayama; Tokyo Governor Ryokichi Minobe; Soka Gakkai president Daisaku Ikeda; Professor Yoshikazu Sakamoto; industrialist and China specialist Kaheita Okazaki; and such diverse personalities within the ruling Liberal-Democratic Party as Aiichiro Fujiyama, Yasuhiro Nakasone, and Tokuma Utsunomiya. Often an interpreter was provided or Japanese friends kindly assisted me. Some of the gentlemen I interviewed were fluent in English. Wherever possible, I checked on the accuracy of controversial statements, sometimes going back to the original source for confirmation. For some of the quotations about the Self-Defense Forces in Chapter 3 I am indebted to the *Mainichi* Newspapers. For a few translated passages on Bushido in Chapter 4 I am grateful to *The East* magazine, and for some textbook material in Chapter 7 I wish to thank *The Japan Times*.

Various friends, professional and personal, have helped me in writing this book. They include Kenkichi Konishi, Yuichiro Kominami, Tom Lewis, Yoko Nagano, Koji Nakamura, John G. Roberts, and Toshiko Suzuki. To these and others, my warmest thanks.

A.A.

Kojimachi, Tokyo
July 1972

Introduction

Many experts on Asia are strongly urging the West, especially the United States, to take a good hard look at what is happening in Japan, the new economic superpower. Some are beginning to worry about a new emerging nationalism in Japan and the possibility of a military comeback.

The dimensions of the problem are huge: the sheer economic might of Japan will enable it to challenge American supremacy in this field, perhaps as early as the 1980's. Much of the problem has to do with Japan's abnormally quick economic growth for over a decade, which has broken all economic speed laws. The history of modern Japan teaches that militarism was cultivated together with economic expansion.

Because of this economic power, it is clear that whichever way Japan goes will have an important impact on much of the world.

One of the West's foremost experts on Japan, Professor Edwin O. Reischauer of Harvard University, said in February, 1972, that the future of the world greatly depends on the future of Japan and on the good relations between Washington and Tokyo. Dr. Reischauer added, in a television interview, that Japan may start a "momentum to a nuclear stance" by the late 1970's. This, he said, would be "most unfortunate." It would be "bad for everybody."

Despite the admonitions, not much is said about the domestic pressures that are building up inside Japan.

In the following pages, I attempt to show that

1. There is a definite resurgence of military strength in Japan.

2. There are strong signs that the ruling elite feels military power is necessary to maintain economic power in the long run.

3. There is very clearly a Japanese military-industrial complex in the making.

4. China and the Soviet Union feel threatened by growing Japanese economic and military power which is viewed favorably, on balance, by Washington.

5. There is a powerful right wing in Japan that has strong appeal to traditional Japanese political and social values, and there is a "value alliance" between the right wing, the political and economic ruling elite, and the military.

6. The left is strong but is at odds both with dominant trends in Japan and, curiously, with many Soviet and Chinese party objectives.

7. The balance of power in Asia is shifting and both the Japanese government and the United States see Japan as a bulwark against Communism.

8. The trend toward the eventual acquisition of self-controlled nuclear weapons by Japan is gaining strength, due to all the above.

9. The movement toward changing the pacifist "Mac-Arthur Constitution" is, therefore, making headway, and a revision may be inevitable.

Chapter 6 deals with the Communist Party and its chances of coming to power through the formation of a left-wing coalition regime. But it ought to be clear at the outset that Japan in the 1970's is neither left nor liberal but archconservative.

It is a country where pacifism is on the decline and police power on the rise. Frequently, one hears Japanese and foreigners as well say that the Japanese probably enjoy too much freedom and democracy and that some abridgment is needed, that morals have become lax and discipline has collapsed. Of course, this may be an exaggeration.

At any rate, the deterioration is not unique to Japan. Other nations suffer similarly. (I sometimes wonder if President Nixon, during his historic trip to Peking, was perhaps filled with envy on observing that city's disciplined citizens, particularly when they all pitched in to shovel snow in the early morning.)

On the whole, Japan's contemporary leadership consists of cautious and prudent men. But behind the scenes are the unreconstructed ultranationalists and militarists, some of whom have not abandoned the belief that Japan has a divine mission in the world. Though the beards of these men are gray, there seems to be a big reservoir of eager young recruits for the ultranationalist camp.

So the question may be asked: Will the more moderate conservative leadership prevail? Or can the zealots make enough noise and create enough disturbances to summon a national emergency?

Then there is the radicalism of the left. Among Japan's left-wing extremists there is a "retrogression theory" to the effect that if enough bombs are thrown, a police state will be revived. This, according to the theory, is when conditions for a revolution will become ripe. But such methods play right into the hands of the ultranationalists, whose power is probably underestimated.

The men in uniform who led Japan during the war appeared ready to commit national suicide. Consider that as late as June 1945 final plans were being readied for a last decisive battle on the Japanese home islands, even if it took the life of every man, woman, and child. Two months later, in a frantic step to prolong the war, some officers tried unsuccessfully to steal the Emperor's recorded message calling on the nation to stop fighting. The atomic bombs had already fallen on Hiroshima and Nagasaki.

That was 1945. In 1970, a popular young member of the National Diet, or Parliament, could make the following statement: "Even if Japan were reduced to ashes it would be able to deal a retaliatory blow to the enemy if it had several MIRV's [multi-warhead missiles] mounted on submarines."

Of course I do not suggest that such an outlook prevails in Japan or is found only in Japan. I merely note its existence in minds that are otherwise presumed to be sober.

A word on the meaning of militarism.

When a state is obviously militaristic, as Japan was under Premier-General Hideki Tojo, it is of course easy to identify. But there may also be degrees of militarism. A country may be partly militaristic; that is, it may lack most of the common elements of militarism but contain one or two of these elements. "Partial militarism" is cited in the authoritative *Dictionary of the Social Sciences* (New York, 1964).

Two trademarks of militarism are a rapidly growing army and an industry that churns out munitions in increasing quantities. Putting the soldier on a pedestal is a component of militarism. Probably so is anti-Communism, although the issue is debatable. In any case, anti-Communism is a thread that runs through all patriotic groups in Japan and is found among all prewar and postwar ultra-nationalistic societies.

The clamor for more territory and a bigger population are factors common to militarism, and some would go so far as to apply the militaristic label to a nation that shows a swift and abnormally large expansion in its overseas markets and investments.

On the left, the Japanese Communist Party has been making inroads into national and local assemblies, and its progress is striking, although it is relative. In terms of seats in the National Diet, for instance, the party remains weak, despite gains in the ten-year period from 1960 to 1970. In 1960, the Communists held six seats in the Diet: three in the lower house and three in the upper house. In 1970, the total Communist seats had increased fourfold, to twenty-four, out of a total number of seats in both houses of the Diet of 741.

Curiously, the extreme left in Japan appears to be counterbalanced by an expanding and militant right wing, which even has its assassination squads. Some members of these squads have already carried out executions. For example, a leading contemporary ultranationalist shot the Prime Minister of Japan at Tokyo Station in 1930. He died a few months later. A teen-aged ultrarightist stabbed to death the chairman of the Japan Socialist Party in 1960 and then took his own life.

The Communists, however, need not entirely despair of ever coming to power. Even such a prominent right-wing theorist as Yoshio Kodama concedes the possibility of a communized Japan—but not before the year 2050.

Finally I wish to make it quite clear that a good deal more could be said about Japan. But the problems raised in the following pages are nonetheless real ones and—given the important position of Japan—deserve the attention of everyone who is interested in the future of Asia and the world.

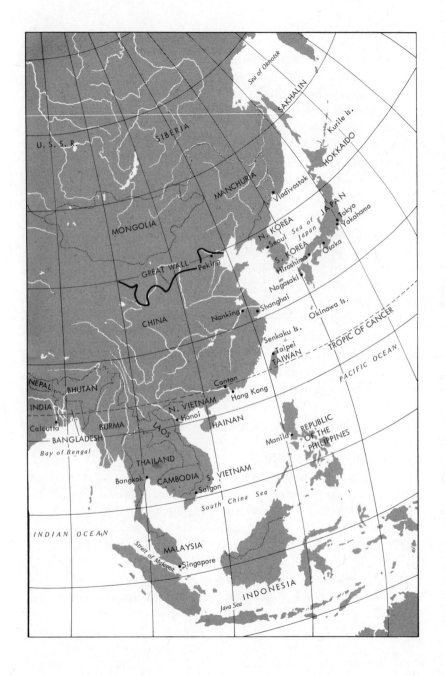

1

Requiem for Pacifism

Before the people become aware of what is happening, Japan might become a militaristic state. . . . Militarism is the greatest danger for Japan.
—Daisaku Ikeda, President of Soka Gakkai, a large Buddhist laymen's organization, interview with author, 1971

Militarism may not be a state of armament alone. It may be just as much a problem of mentality, a state of mind. I strongly feel China's charges of militarism are largely directed against the social climate of Japan, which is susceptible to totalitarianism.
—Aiichiro Fujiyama, former Foreign Minister of Japan, interview with Koji Nakamura and author, 1971

For years, everyone has marveled at Japan's ability to do what was thought impossible: to transform itself from a beaten and ravaged nation, with its people crammed into four rather rock-ribbed islands, into an affluent nation. Japan, which lacks many natural resources, has become the third richest country on earth. This vast accumulation of wealth and prosperity goes on, although the record-breaking pace has slowed. But while this giant's growth looks less, its actual economic expansion each year is enormous.

Now there is a vague but menacing apprehension. Japan, once regarded as meek, pacifist, and militarily naked, is rearming. Some observers note a bit of swaggering, although this may be entirely natural and understandable with the new national self-confidence that is everywhere noticeable. It is not precisely known which path Japan, now an economic superpower, will follow in the years ahead. The country is perhaps the least predictable of the major powers. On this, many experts agree.

The fact is that Japan is seeking, and is no doubt entitled to, a much wider role in world affairs as well as real equality with its closest ally and foremost trading partner, the United States. Japan has already entered into a position where it is now able to exploit its superior industrial and technological strength for political ends whenever it chooses.

Japanese eyes are cast especially on Southeast Asia, a region of vast natural resources which is doubtless of greater economic and political concern for Japan than any other country. Presently, Southeast Asia accounts for about one-fourth, or $9.5 billion, of Japan's total world trade. In addition, it seems that no other people exhibit more nervousness than the Japanese over the real or imagined security vacuum developing in that region because of the steady cuts in the number of American and British forces there. If, as some experts maintain, the future of the Malacca Strait is uncertain, no one is more conscious of it than Japan, whose commercial life lines pass through the strait and cross the Indian Ocean to the rich oil fields surrounding the Persian Gulf.

The main question is whether Japan, in its indomitable quest for equality and a world-leadership role as befits its industrial ranking, will also seek great military power, including nuclear weapons. Denials by Tokyo officials, as well as by various foreign experts on Japan, that the country will ever again become militaristic are not entirely reassuring.

In Japan, there are sporadic demands that the nation acquire nuclear arms. Many experts say a Japanese drive to obtain nuclear weapons could prove the most dangerous policy of all.

Tokyo has a well-subsidized space program and is doing considerable research in rocketry, missiles, and nuclear energy for peaceful purposes. Japan has already launched a civilian nuclear-powered vessel. It has joined that select group of nations which has lofted artificial satellites into space. Because of Japan's developments in rocketry, some experts say Japan will have a workable nuclear-weapons delivery system long before its possible possession of nuclear weapons.

The issues of rearmament and nuclear weapons are controversial in Japan and they are being debated with increasing frequency. One question that is often heard is: Can Japan really be independent if it continues to ask another nation to shoulder part of its defense? Under the Treaty of Mutual Security with the United States, Washington has assumed obligations to defend Japan against aggression. Leftists naturally wish to jettison the military alliance with the United States, but a majority of the citizens probably also feel uneasy about it.

Although not so critical of the alliance as the left, the right wing also sees some advantages in reducing or completely eliminating Japan's military dependence on America. The thinking is that the people would probably be more agreeable to a major expansion of the Self-Defense Forces if a big reduction took place in U.S. military bases in Japan. Presently, there are about ninety U.S. installations in Japan, not including Okinawa.

Another question that is often asked is: Should Japan remain under the American nuclear umbrella? An increasing number of Japanese, including many liberals, have begun to doubt the effectiveness of this protection, even though most Japanese citizens view nuclear weapons as anathema.

At the present time, Japan is rearming quietly without going through the politically painful process of amending the pacifist Constitution under which rearmament is illegal.

Accompanying this quiet rearmament is the rising defense budget in Japan, which is a very important trend. Japan is now in the midst of its fourth five-year defense build-up plan (1972–76). The cost of this plan is double the third, which was double the second, which was roughly double the first.

Specifically, the first defense build-up plan cost almost $2 billion; the second cost $3.6 billion; and the third $7 billion. By the time the fourth plan is completed, in 1976, the total cost is likely to be $16 billion, or a minimum of $3 billion each year. Some Japanese military analysts predict the fifth defense build-up plan will run between $25 billion and $30 billion. They also suspect that expenditures for nuclear-arms development may be included in the sixth build-up plan (1982–86), if not the fifth. In any case, it may be said that Japan's defense budgets are showing a tendency toward boundless growth.

In the early 1970's, Japan's military budget was hovering near 1 per cent of the nation's gross national product. This figure looked as if it would double by the end of the fourth build-up period and perhaps even triple by the close of this decade. The percentage of the GNP for the military seemed small. After all, in the same period (1971–72) it was tiny compared with the United States (7%), Russia (12%), China (8.5%), and Britain, France, and West Germany (each near 5%).

But it should be noted that Japan's GNP was the third largest in the world, and it was expected to rise to between $300 billion and $400 billion within six years.

Moreover, the military spending of these other powers, with the exception of West Germany, included large sums for nuclear forces.

Japan's total defense outlay in 1972 was about half of West Germany's. But West Germany had 100,000 more men in its army than Japan. It must also be remembered that West Germany has land boundaries with no fewer than nine countries, including Czechoslovakia and East

Germany. By contrast, Japan's borders are absolute: next to them are only deep seas or channels.

Some critics charge that the Japanese defense build-up already goes beyond mere requirements for self-defense. The charge is immeasurably hard to prove. Nevertheless, Japanese government officials have frankly stated that Japan must have enough retaliatory power to strike back at enemy bases if an attack is launched against Japan. Meanwhile, the continuing defense build-up is creating doubt in the minds of some nations that Japan's military may not always remain defensive in character.

In the same vein, various neighboring nations are growing suspicious of Japanese proposals, usually informally made, to dispatch Japanese peacekeeping forces overseas to help other nations in an emergency, or to train military units of other countries that are friendly to Japan.

Japanese military officers say the Self-Defense Forces have seven or eight times the firepower of the defunct Imperial forces at the peak of their fighting excellence, around 1942. This means that individually, the Japanese soldier of today packs from seven to eight times the wallop of his 1942 counterpart.

This military strength is accelerating.

Japan's navy, or Maritime Self-Defense Force, will build approximately a hundred warships of all descriptions under the fourth five-year plan. These ships will add about 100,000 tons to the navy, which is to total 320,000 tons by 1981. That figure is roughly equal to the tonnage of the Japanese Imperial Navy in 1905 when it destroyed the Imperial Russian fleet in the battle of Tsushima.

By any standard, such a naval build-up goes beyond mere coastal defense, which was supposed to be the rationale for the maritime force. Few would deny that Japan, a

major power, needs adequate defense strength. Its forces
are up-to-date and are being equipped with automatic
weapons and missiles. New armament, such as Phantom
jet fighters and attack submarines, which are capable of
engaging an enemy outside the nation's territorial waters,
have been added.

But the catch is that the government has rather sur-
reptitiously built up its postwar military forces, even keeping up the fiction that they do not constitute armed forces.
This was done to circumvent the Constitution as well as
the pacifist resistance of the citizenry. Hence, the resort to
euphemism: Self-Defense Forces, which probably reveals
an official guilty conscience. The authorities still hesitate
to say that Japan has armed forces.

In fact, the naming of the military has been a recurring
problem. First it was National Police Reserve (1950); then,
National Safety Force (1952); then, Self-Defense Force
(1954). Possibly, the name will see another change in the
future.

The Constitution, of course, says nothing about a Self-
Defense Force or any force. Many Japanese still retain unpleasant memories of police forces, especially the "thought-
control police" of the prewar and wartime epochs.

On top of all this, the Defense Agency, sometimes jok-
ingly called Japan's mini-Pentagon, has ruled out an invasion of Japan by sea. However, since an invasion could
not possibly take place except by sea, an invasion of Japan
would thus seem to be ruled out altogether. In this connection, a glance at history is helpful: no invasion of Japan
has occurred since the Mongols tried it in the thirteenth
century and failed dismally when a "divine wind" sent
their invasion fleet to the bottom.

Professor Reischauer says Japanese rearmament could,

in time, lead to an unwholesome rivalry with the Soviet Union and the United States. But he believes the greatest tensions would be created between Japan and China. A look at Far Eastern politics shows that these tensions already exist.

Of the three nations mentioned—China, Russia, and America—China is the only one with whom Japan has not yet opened diplomatic relations. Despite many individual friendships between Japanese and Chinese, the Sino-Japanese legacy of fighting, friction, intrigue, and mistrust has yet to be replaced by a new era of amity and cooperation.

A number of critics say many of the above developments are premonitory signs that Japan is leaning hard toward becoming a future military power. If so, there are many additional signs that may be noted.

The intimacy between Japan's arms manufacturers and the nation's military is beginning to disturb not just the overly sensitive. Japan's weapons industry is being rebuilt, and its leaders constantly prod the government to ease the present limits on weapons exports, even though they are somewhat flexible. In 1971 the Stockholm International Peace Research Institute listed Japan as an "arms-exporting nation." Of course, Japan was only a minor exporter. Its annual total arms sales came to less than $10 million. But already some persons close to the U.S. government have raised the possibility that Japan may replace the United States as the chief supplier of arms for Asia.

Japan has had ample postwar experience in this field. At the outbreak of the Korean War in 1950, Japan became what was called the workshop of Asia and the Far Eastern arsenal of the Free World. At the beginning of 1951, almost three-fourths of Japanese production was directly engaged in what was known as defense production, says Professor Chitoshi Yanaga of Yale. In 1952, during the Korean War but after Japan had regained its independence, plants that had been earmarked for reparations were returned to their owners. These included 314 aircraft factories, 25 weapons and air-research centers, 19 steel mills, 19 machine-tool-manufacturing plants, 18 shipyards, 6 synthetic-rubber factories, and 131 military arsenals.

Actually, given such countries as South Vietnam, South Korea, and Taiwan with their armies of half a million men or more, plus other areas which also have seemingly endless problems of insurgency, the prospects for lucrative Japanese weapons sales appear to be excellent.

Some Japanese industrialists advocate total rearmament. Moreover, there is the belief, and it appears to have become part of established policy, that Japan must wield greater military power to cope with its new economic status in the world. Not surprisingly, such an idea has given rise to an inchoate fear by Asian nations who remember the prewar Greater East Asia Co-prosperity Sphere—the cloak used for Japan's territorial expansion—and the excesses committed in upholding it.

Some Japanese business leaders and politicians, too, go further. They say Japan will be abused by others if it lacks nuclear weapons. They believe the time has come to speak up in support of nuclearization.

Meanwhile, the Japanese Defense Agency has let it be known that it is interested in launching a nuclear-driven warship or two. The government, for its part, has said that Japan has the right to detonate peaceful nuclear devices if it wishes. So far, it has not wanted to do so. But Japanese officials claim, not without a bit of swagger, that Japan is a nuclear-capable nation.

When Japan does decide that it wants nuclear arms, it

will be able to produce them quickly. Japan is what is known as a threshold nation—a nation technically capable of making the bomb. The country could produce the bomb within two years. It has both the funds and the technology to do so.

Yet the very idea of nuclearization disturbs many citizens. The government, according to various Japanese observers, is attempting to wear down the people's aversion to nuclear weapons gradually. In fact, conservative phrasemakers have thought up the clever expression "nuclear allergy" to disparage the general fear and distaste for nuclear arms.

If Japan is bent on remaining a non-nuclear power, its actions may seem paradoxical. Japan has steadfastly refused to ratify the treaty which bans the spread of nuclear weapons, the Nuclear Nonproliferation Treaty. Japan signed the treaty in 1970 but balks at ratification, claiming the treaty would make Japan a permanent second-class nation.

The treaty has also been damned as an "unequal treaty." The term is historic and evocative. It was widely used in Japan during the ultranationalistic 1920's and 1930's when the Japanese military, with much public support, demanded naval parity with the major Western powers. When the naval-limitations conferences in Washington (1922) and London (1930) gave an approximate ratio of 5:5:3 in naval tonnage to America, Britain, and Japan, however, many Japanese felt angry and humiliated. Among the nation's young military officers, this unequal naval apportionment was an outstanding grievance. These same officers plotted one *coup d'état* after another in alliance with civilian ultranationalists in the 1930's.

One military man, Admiral Isoroku Yamamoto, who

took part in the naval limitation talks and later com-
manded the Imperial Fleet in 1941, expressed his feelings
strongly: "I was never told that being shorter than the
other delegates at London I ought to eat only three-fifths
of the food on my plate."

Shortly before the jingoist novelist, Yukio Mishima, committed ritual hara-kiri in 1970, he fumed against the Nuclear Nonproliferation Treaty as a replay of the "5:5:3 unequal treaty of former years." Mishima spoke of "gnashing
our teeth" while waiting for the nation's samurai ideals to
rise again.

If the aversion to nuclear weapons is lessening, pacifism
is also on the wane. At one time after World War II, when
there was widespread revulsion to all forms of militarism,
pacifism was doubtless the most popular "ism" in Japan.
Members of the U.S. Occupation Forces who landed in
Japan in late 1945 were stunned to discover how firmly
pacifism had taken root among the people. Even before
the Occupation Forces arrived, the Ministry of Education
had told students to "dry your tears and please return to
gentleness." It was a fine contrast to General Hideki Tojo's
wartime injunction to youth to "break and throw away
your pens."

The Japanese had ample reason to abhor war. Almost
2 million soldiers had fallen. The remains of tens of thousands of them still lie in foreign lands and subtropical
islands. (A photograph in *The New York Times* on March
15, 1972, shows the skulls and bones of Japanese war dead
being burned in Saipan in observation of traditional rites.
Some ten thousand Japanese soldiers died defending that
Pacific island alone in 1944.) Everybody knows that Hiroshima and Nagasaki were destroyed. But other Japanese
cities suffered as much or more destruction from air raids.

For example, about 89 per cent of Nagoya was destroyed, and Osaka lost almost 60 per cent of its houses. Tokyo lost over 1 million houses or apartment buildings.

The people's loathing for the war showed itself in their wide endorsement of the new pacifist Constitution, even though the document was largely the handiwork of aliens. Democracy as set forth in the Constitution and as a central policy of the U.S. Occupation won an enthusiastic response from the Japanese people. Women were given voting rights for the first time. All citizens were granted more freedoms than they had ever enjoyed before. However, it should not be thought that democracy was a completely alien import. There were some important indigenous democratic trends in Japan, especially in the Meiji Era (1868–1912) and in the 1920's.

Although pacifism thrived after World War II ended, it received some very hard blows from the Korean War and, later, from America's involvement in Indochina. It was, incidentally, the Korean War and the departure of U.S. soldiers stationed in Japan for the Korean battlefields which led to establishment of a National Police Reserve, the forerunner of the Self-Defense Forces. American military bases in Japan and Okinawa and the existence of the military alliance between Washington and Tokyo made the Indochina War especially a matter of extreme urgency and controversy for the Japanese.

It was perhaps natural that some traditionalist-minded Japanese despised the aftermath of the Pacific War, which saw a breakdown of family ties and many of the old values. They longed for the bygone days of the Empire. Some still do. Hundreds of thousands of Japanese are living today who once served in China, Korea, and other areas before World War II, as soldiers, bureaucrats, businessmen, or

technicians. In the early 1930's, Japanese-controlled territory, including the Japanese home islands, totaled nearly
500,000 square miles. By 1942 this territory had expanded
to more than 3,044,000 square miles, or an area larger than
the United States without Alaska and the Hawaiian Islands. Today, Japan's domain is limited to four main
islands with an area of 142,812 square miles.

Curiously, it was during the worldwide depression of
the early thirties that many Japanese came to associate
democracy, pacifism, and free enterprise with their appalling economic conditions, and they quite willingly listened to advocates of militarism and ultranationalism. The
chief propaganda agents at this time were members of the
superpatriotic societies.

After Japan's defeat in 1945, many of the former militarists and ultranationalists went into hibernation for a
few years, only to emerge after the U.S. Occupation ended.
Then a rather sensational event occurred in the mid-1960's
which tended to strengthen the ultranationalist movement
greatly. At one fell swoop, the most notorious underworld
gangs united with major rightist groups into one big family called Kantokai. This union is not really so strange as
it sounds, because many of Japan's underworld figures have
one foot in politics. Moreover, with few exceptions they
are rabid nationalists and anti-Communists.

The guiding hand behind this alliance was Yoshio
Kodama, probably the foremost rightist theorist in Japan.
A fund raiser and political manipulator, he operated the
Kodama Organ in China during the war, which helped to
obtain an uninterrupted flow of supplies to the Imperial
Navy. Kodama frankly admits that the basic tenets of ultra-
nationalism in Japan lead straight to militarism.

Ever since Japan regained its sovereignty, many of the

key politicians in the nation have been the very same persons who appeared in the wartime cabinets or who held other important wartime posts in government and industry. Among them are Nobusuke Kishi and Okinori Kaya, who served as ministers in the Tojo Cabinet and, after confinement as war criminals, rose to power in the postwar era. Kishi became Prime Minister (1957–60) while Kaya became Justice Minister (1963–64). Kishi later became president of the America-Japan society. If such comebacks startle foreigners, they also evoke disapproval from many Japanese, including a few ruling party politicians.

Some particularly stern critics call Kishi and Kaya "our totalitarian elders." One such critic is Tokuma Utsunomiya, an outspoken member of the ruling Liberal-Democratic Party, who offers this tart comment: "What makes me angry is the fact that the Greater East Asia War was started by totalitarians and that these same totalitarians are now calling themselves democratically-minded and are even now preparing Japan for another war." The independent-minded Utsunomiya, the son of an Imperial army general, is often at odds with the ruling party leadership.

Another critic, Shunsuke Tsurumi, a professor at Doshisha University in Kyoto, finds it a strange thing that these and similar men, who supported the Japanese drive in China, are still in power. But what is more strange, he observes, is that most Japanese no longer feel the incongruity of it. This, says Dr. Tsurumi, constitutes "unreasonableness" in Japanese society.

When contemporary right-wing politicians speak their minds, one often hears echos of the past. For example, militant leaders of the 1930's employed a shrewd vocabulary of life lines. First they said Manchuria was vital to Japan's national interests. So Japan made Manchuria into a puppet state, called Manchukuo. These vital interests were then enlarged to embrace other parts of China and later, a large part of Southeast Asia.

Nowadays, the most conservative of leaders stress the need to defend the maritime life line of Japan which, they claim, passes close to Taiwan and through the Malacca Strait, the strategic channel that connects the South China Sea with the Indian Ocean. This is sometimes referred to as the Malacca Strait Defense Line.

About 90 per cent of the oil that feeds Japan's industries is shipped through the Malacca Strait—sometimes Japanese tankers pass through at five-minute intervals—and it is said that if this oil flow were suddenly stopped, the Japanese economy would be stifled within a month. But the fact is that no great power has threatened or is threatening to close the strait. China, if it were so inclined, does not have the warships to do it. In addition, it is apparent that if China or the Soviet Union were at war with Japan, the danger to Japan's industrial sinews would be of much closer proximity than the Malacca Strait.

The Soviets do have a naval presence in the Indian Ocean. So does the United States. In fact, the Pentagon is said to be constructing a permanent naval base on Britain's Diego Garcia Island, a thousand miles south of India, which is scheduled for completion in 1973.

Smaller powers could make trouble. Indonesia and Malaya have asserted the right to regulate traffic through the strait, perhaps even subjecting ships to tolls. But they would hardly think of closing it. Japan is a vital market for both nations, and, in addition, provides important loans and investments, plus various forms of technological aid.

Interestingly, it was reported in 1972 that although Japan had reasonably offered to help deepen the Malacca Strait in order to permit supertankers to pass without danger, it had "acted so heavy-handedly that it seemed some degree of Japanese control would sneak in the side door." The words are from an April 10, 1972, column in *Newsweek* by William P. Bundy, former U.S. Assistant Secretary of State for Far Eastern Affairs.

There is another Japanese life line: the 38th parallel that divides North and South Korea. It is often called the first line of Japanese defense by officers of the Self-Defense Forces as well as military analysts and various politicians. Some of them speak of the Red Flag at Pusan Theory. This theory maintains that if South Korea is communized, Japan will soon be caught in the same net. Pusan is the major South Korean port city in the southern tip of that country, about 120 miles from Japan. At the time of the greatest advance by the Communists during the Korean War, Pusan remained within the small perimeter of land that was not overrun by the enemy.

Are these notions of life lines perhaps signs of renascent Japanese ambition? Some observers say yes; others explain that it is only natural for a strong nation with massive industrial power to do whatever is required to protect its trade and other interests.

Japan may be said to have taken a first step in seeking to protect its economic interests in Asia. By agreement with the United States, Japan publicly stated in a joint communiqué, signed in November 1969, that both South Korea and Taiwan were important to Japan's security. Some observers interpreted the document to mean that Tokyo and Washington were acknowledging these lands to be within Japan's sphere of influence. Both South Korea and Taiwan are former colonies of Japan. Taiwan, doubtless, is the most prickly part of the Japan-China problem.

Those who follow Far Eastern politics closely are fairly well agreed that the relations between Tokyo and Peking will have a very important bearing on the rise of Japanese military power. Actually, rivalry with China appears to be taken for granted in Japanese military policy.

Japan's military leaders, together with some conservative politicians, have hypothesized China as the most probable future enemy of Japan. China's name is even written down in several hypothetical war plans drawn up by the Defense Agency, including those referred to as Three Arrows and Flying Dragon. The Soviet Union was also listed as an enemy in these plans, which were somehow leaked to the Japan Socialist Party, which disclosed their contents in the National Diet. The Soviets, who have diplomatic ties with Tokyo, protested. As a result, Japanese officials (who were terribly embarrassed by the entire disclosure) said they had instructed the Defense Agency to delete the name of the Soviet Union from the plans. This apparently placated the Kremlin.

The Defense Agency, with eyes especially cocked on events in China, has said that the offensive capability of China must be taken into account in Japan's military build-up. According to the Agency, China will have eighty to a hundred intermediate-range ballistic missiles, plus about ten intercontinental ballistic missiles, by 1976. The Pentagon has also warned that China will become a nuclear-missile threat in the late 1970's and 1980's. It has said that China will have between ten and twenty ICBM's in the late 1970's. On military matters, Tokyo and Washington often use the same spectacles.

Does the failure to apologize for the hurt one nation has done to another reveal an aspect of militarism? China says yes. The Chinese are still waiting for Japan to make an official apology for the barbarism of its soldiers on the China mainland. But Japanese government leaders have persistently refused; nor are they about to sign a peace treaty with Peking. They say the treaty Japan entered into with Generalissimo Chiang Kai-shek's Nationalist regime in 1952 put an end to the war with China.

Those who recall the misery of war or annexation and insist that Japan show true remorse include not only the Chinese. Korean scholar Dr. Yu Jin Oh, former president of Korean University in Seoul, says: "The people of Korea have long wanted Japan's leaders to say, 'We were wrong and we apologize.' Instead, a Japanese Foreign Minister [Etsusaburo Shiina] came to Seoul and said, 'We will search our hearts'—but not, 'We were wrong and we apologize.' "

In 1971 the Prime Minister of Japan, Eisaku Sato (younger brother of Nobusuke Kishi), addressed the Diet in these words: "What is the background for China often attacking the revival of militarism in Japan? I would like to consider this question." Sato continued: "I believe that the scars left behind by the Japanese military faction in China cannot be healed. I will meditate frankly on the past." But, like the Koreans, the Chinese do not accept meditation as a substitute for apology.

Takeo Fukuda, when he was Foreign Minister of Japan, said on December 16, 1971, that "concerning the suffering inflicted on China in the Sino-Japanese war, the first precondition is that Japan apologize." No doubt Japan will apologize. But many will wonder why it took so long to utter the words.

What of the Japanese people? Do they feel remorse over the war against China and other Asian peoples? Yes, they do, and they have shown it in a myriad of ways. But they feel strongly, and justifiably, that they also were victims of the war and of militarism. And, of course, it was Japan that felt atomic bombs with its own flesh.

The Japanese have given war reparations to a number of Southeast Asian countries and also to South Korea. These reparations, given in yen or in yen credits, have proved to be a boon to the Japanese economy. The Chinese, who suffered greatly from the Japanese, have received nothing. (When Tokyo signed a peace treaty with Taipei, Chiang Kai-shek, who controlled only Taiwan, waived any reparations from Japan.) It may be of interest to note that the Federal Republic of Germany has given large-scale compensation to many of the victims of Nazi Germany, including restitution to individuals and survivors of those who were murdered. In addition, the West Germans have taken over from the Allies the prosecution of Nazi crimes, and they have done this fairly conscientiously. The Germans have striven to make amends for the past. In the Orient, some Asians rebuke Japan for not going far enough in atoning for the war with China and other Asian countries.

The wartime experiences of Japan's older generation are, meanwhile, fading rapidly. When, early in 1972, a World War II soldier was discovered on Guam and brought home after hiding out for twenty-seven years in the steamy jungles, he received a rousing welcome. Instead of feeling lucky to be alive, the holdout said: "I came home alive, of which I feel very much ashamed." Many persons admired the old-time patriotism this statement represented.

A whole new generation has appeared since 1945 which

never knew war or suffering. It is almost a third of the population—35 million men and women. Many, of course, belong to the leftist or liberal camp. They have joined demonstrations against the U.S. involvement in the Indochina War, and the Japanese government's support of the American role. They oppose rearmament. On the other hand, there are also many young people who are attracted by a new surge of nationalism and patriotism.

As rearmament goes on, the people are showing increasing apathy toward politics, a risky business in a democracy.

Instead, there is preoccupation with the complexities and insecurities of life, especially urban life, with its mobility, pollution, noise, overcrowding, lack of privacy, and increased violence. Nor can these problems be considered without mentioning the business of making a living. In December 1971, Japan expert Professor Herbert Passin of Columbia University observed in an interview with *The New York Times* that political stability in Japan was being severely shaken by social mobility, especially the rapid movement of a large part of the farm population to the cities.

When a breadwinner has a spare minute, he wants to relax, watch television, or read a magazine. Television, many of my Japanese friends would agree, is no less idiotic in Japan than in any other presumably advanced country. It is also full of violence. In 1971 the National Diet received the following grim report from a conservative lawmaker. He said that on a Sunday television "golden hour"—between 8 P.M. and 9 P.M.—forty-two persons were either cut or stabbed. Also, in three hours, starting at 6 P.M., there were 509 beatings, shootings, and free-for-alls on the television screen. (In March 1972, Dr. Jesse L. Steinfeld, the U.S. Surgeon General, told a congressional committee in Washington, D.C., that there was sufficient data to establish a causal relationship between watching TV violence and aggressive behavior.)

Newsstands in Japan sag under the weight of 750 million copies of magazines published each year—a world record. Dozens of sexy magazines and comic books, some an inch thick, provide weekly reading material for young men and women. It is a kind of mind pollution.

Despite the fact that Japan's 105 million people are living in an area the size of California, the government not long ago called for an increase in the birth rate. The cynics were suspicious even though the reason given was an acute labor shortage. There had been talk in the Diet about importing large numbers of Korean workers to fill the gap in the production lines, but the idea was rejected because it posed political problems. In March 1970, Professor Minoru Tachi, who was director of the Ministry of Health and Welfare's Institute of Population Problems, said that "Japan already has the highest actual population density in the world." In 1971 Japan's density of population per square mile was about 725. By comparison, the United States had 57, Britain 589, and West Germany 622.

In the 1930's, Japanese leaders talked about being an overcrowded nation in need of additional space. Japan's population was then around 75 million. The saturation point was put at 90 million. Japan now has 15 million more people than that.

How do the overcrowded Japanese people feel about the problem of militarism?

An opinion poll in October 1971 probably portrays the people's fears accurately. The poll, by the respected *Yomiuri Shimbun,* with samples taken in all of Japan's 46 prefectures, showed that half the people (actually 49.8%) believed militarism has been or is being revived.

What is important is that, five years previously, few if any polls were taken on the subject of militarism in Japan. Now there are many. The very idea of a military comeback in the 1960's seemed farfetched. Some editorial writers termed it an impossibility. Now, real fears have been awakened.

Many Japanese put the Okinawa problem and the issue of militarism together. Opinion polls show the 1 million Okinawans, who lived for a quarter of a century under U.S. military rule, favored demilitarization of their island before it was returned to Japanese control in 1972. Instead, the Ryukyu Islands, of which Okinawa is the largest, continue to support about one hundred military bases and other facilities. Military bases account for approximately 12 per cent of the land area of Okinawa.

To Okinawans, their island has an even greater military coloring now than before because of the introduction of small units of the Self-Defense Forces in addition to the remaining Americans. The citizens, while not enamored of a foreign military presence, seem even less kindly disposed toward new platoons of Japanese soldiers. The reason has much to do with World War II, when the Japanese military men forced many civilians to kill themselves to leave more food for the Imperial Army.* In addition, the Okinawans know the Americans will go home eventually. But

---

* In 1970, an ex-officer of the Imperial Army who wanted to return to one of the islands near Okinawa was recognized and denied entry with the challenge: "Why are you still alive?" It turned out he had ordered the deaths of many civilians during the last days of the Battle of Okinawa in June 1945.

they believe the Self-Defense Forces will grow bigger on Okinawa and will never depart. The Okinawans are, once again, pawns of history, according to a former U.S. diplomat in Tokyo, John K. Emmerson, who expects rough times ahead for both Japan and America on the Okinawa problem.

The Americans are not going to depart soon, either. They have begun a $60 million base construction project to last through 1976. In 1970 the Pentagon allotted nearly $200,000 alone for a sentry-dog training center to be built on Okinawa. Observers said this indicated the U.S. forces planned to be on Okinawa for a long time.

Meanwhile, there is an Irredentist movement in Japan. The nation already has laid claim to the formerly American-controlled Senkaku Islands situated between Okinawa and Taiwan. Both Taiwan and China say these small islands are Chinese territory. However, Tokyo has made preparations to control the islands militarily. In addition, there is a drive to repossess the Kurile Islands in the north, which the Soviets seized from Japan at the end of World War II. The country that owns these islands obtains a strategic advantage over shipping and fishing in the northern Pacific, one of the richest sources of sea food in the world.

However, when questioned as to the problem of militarism, government and ruling party leaders are unequivocal: Japan will never again revert to a militarist-type state. It is impossible, they assert. However, they do admit the historical fact that no great economic power has remained intact without also becoming a great military power. "We will be different," say Japan's leaders.

To refrain from being a great military power is a "stupendous task," Prime Minister Sato said in 1970, "but we will do it."

The 1970 White Paper on Defense also is emphatic: "The Japanese nation will become a great power in an economic sense but never in a military sense."

The White Paper also contained this paragraph, which repays reading:

The re-evaluation of the Self-Defense Forces as a vehicle for people's education, as a place for application of their education, and as an instrument of social experience, the establishment of correct relationships between them, and enabling the Self-Defense Forces and the industrial world to have proper relations of mutual interdependence and relations of mutually assisting each other's development; all these factors must be said to be extremely important in the 1970's with manpower shortage, development of science and technology, and the build-up of defense capabilities.

This emphasis on the nation's armed forces as a "vehicle for people's education" and of "mutual interdependence" between industry and the military provides a good insight into the thinking of national leaders who are vigorously backing stepped-up rearmament.

2
The New Zaibatsu

The Japanese have dedicated themselves to be-
coming the biggest manufacturing nation in the
world. . . . The only thing that must be watched
is the link between the government and business
in Japan. Business is government-guided and the
two act as a group. They have a planned arrange-
ment that gives them great strength. . . . This
is a system that does not usually exist outside to-
talitarian countries, and certainly not in Aus-
tralia and the U.S.

> —E. T. Hamilton, president, U.S. Chamber
> of Commerce in Australia, remarks made in
> December 1970

Japan's efforts to concentrate on domestic pro-
duction of arms along the lines of "independent
self-defense" will likely lead to narrow-minded
nationalism.

> —Hiroshi Osanai, military affairs analyst,
> quoted by Dr. Yoshikazu Sakamoto in *Asahi*
> *Shimbun,* 1971

Daubs of war paint have begun to appear on the faces of the *zaibatsu,* or money cliques, the industrial colossi that once produced some of the world's biggest battleships, like the *Yamato* and *Musashi,* and also submarines, bombers, and the Zero fighter.

These firms are in the vanguard of Japanese rearmament. They are even supplying sophisticated armaments to the United States, including gun sights for Phantom jet fighter-bombers, homing torpedoes, a new type radar for weapons systems, and an advanced 20 mm. cannon for aircraft. The fact is, a partial militarization of Japan's quarter trillion dollar economy has occurred, and its tempo is quickening.

Armaments production, though small, already plays a vital role in certain fields of production in Japan's super economy, such as aircraft manufacturing. It depends on military orders for as much as 80 per cent of its business.

Mitsubishi Heavy Industries (MHI), together with other zaibatsu, such as Kawasaki Heavy Industries and Fuji Heavy Industries, have reckoned on defense contracts through 1976 big enough to enable them to triple their aircraft sales. At its Nagoya aircraft works, Mitsubishi has been developing supersonic jet trainers for the Defense Agency. Fuji Heavy Industries, Nissan Motors, and Tokyo Shibaura Electric (Toshiba) have joined forces to manufacture ship-to-ship missiles. It is being whispered that MHI, a part of the Mitsubishi group, would like to take over the former world position of Rolls-Royce by going

into the manufacture of large-size jet engines, primarily
for military use.

Mitsubishi's role in the nation's rearmament is huge. Between 1965 and 1970, MHI—sometimes called the Krupp
of the Orient—took the lion's share, or about 46 per cent,
of major defense contracts awarded to a handful of industrial giants. The Mitsubishi group of over forty corporations* controls a third of Japan's defense industry. It is
doubtless a world's record. Probably no other single group
of firms anywhere in the non-Communist world controls a
third of a major country's defense industry and not only
builds warships, tanks, and missiles but also aspires to make
both the fuselage and large engines of jet aircraft for military use.

Kaoru Murakami, a leading Japanese military commen-
tator, compares weapons production to a cancer cell. "Once
weapons production takes root in an enterprise, it will
never shrink." He adds: "When I examine Mitsubishi's
moves, I feel it is already in a pre-cancer state."

The basic defense budget for the 1972–76 build-up is
approximately $16 billion, or double the former five-year
plan. Despite some initial cuts, it is not likely to be reduced in the end. Small wonder that big business supports
military build-up, supports an expanded security role for
Japan in the Far East, and generally favors future possession of nuclear weapons. In 1969, Kogoro Uemura, one of
Japan's most powerful industrialists, told *Keidanren* (Federation of Economic Organizations) that a collective security system for Japan was "an international responsibility

---

* In *Fortune* magazine's 1971 list of the two hundred largest corporations
outside the United States, Japan became for the first time the most heavily
represented country on the list; fifty-one companies were Japanese, including six Mitsubishi firms.

and an important problem connected with Japan's future prosperity." Japan, he said, had the duty to contribute to maintenance of peace in Asia. This idea happens to be part of the basic philosophy behind the U.S.-Japan military alliance.

Some of the outspoken Japanese hawks are zaibatsu officials who eagerly adapt the idea of big military build-up "commensurate with the nation's economic strength." They plump for a large navy to patrol the high seas and to defend the Malacca Strait from possible blockade.

Representative statements from a couple of Mitsubishi hawks who have spoken their minds demonstrate this support. Ken Okubo, president of Mitsubishi Electric Corporation and a past president of the Japan Weapons Industry Association, says bluntly that he is a militarist. He believes Japan should quadruple its military spending. It is forecast that Japan's gross national product may rise to as much as $400 billion by the late 1970's. If Japan's defense expenditures remained at only 1 per cent of the GNP, this would blossom to $4 billion. Merely to double the percentage, then, would mean $8 billion for defense for one year. This amount would likely surpass the defense spending by all of the major West European powers. And competent observers say it will probably come to pass in the latter part of the 1970's. Okubo also urges Japanese possession of atomic arms on the grounds that the nation can be neither secure nor equal to the other major powers until it, too, controls such weapons.

The zaibatsu desire for nuclear weapons is constant and becomes more emphatic with time. Industrialists, in addition to the military, assert that a nation's technology is greatly enhanced by weapons research, and in the atomic age this is even more true for research on nuclear weapons.

It follows logically that a nation lacking such weapons may fall behind in the most advanced technology. This is one reason sometimes heard for Japan's failure to ratify the treaty for nonproliferation of nuclear weapons. (Sweden told the Geneva Disarmament Conference in 1972 that the treaty prohibiting the spread of nuclear weapons had entered a kind of twilight zone because nations technically capable of making the bomb, like Japan, had failed to ratify it.) It is also the thinking of a growing number of Japanese industrialists.

Interest by the zaibatsu in nuclear energy is shown in many ways.

Japan will no doubt be launching a number of nuclear-powered ships, including warships, by the early 1980's or before. The Defense Agency is eager to build SSN's (nuclear-powered submarines) and has already compiled technical data on the use of nuclear fuel for submarines. The Japan Atomic Industrial Council has predicted the nation will build no fewer than 280 nuclear-driven ships before the century closes. The Council said Japan would build two nuclear-powered merchant ships by 1980, fifty to sixty by 1990, and 280 by the year 2000. A few military experts predict that the fifth build-up plan (1977–81) will include at least one SSN. The plan is expected to cost a minimum of $25 billion.

The zaikai, the inner sanctum of Japanese industry and finance that governs Japan, has given broad hints of things to come. Zai in Japanese means money, kai means circles. Put together, the two words stand for about thirty men, mostly in banking, iron and steel, and electric power. Kazutaka Kikawada, president of Tokyo Electric Power Corporation, seeks guarantees for the security of the Malacca Strait, Ken Okubo not only wants a larger defense budget, he wants naval tonnage trebled. Industrialist Take-shi Sakurada wants to revoke Article 9 of the Constitution so military forces may be sent abroad.

Chujiro Fujino, president of Mitsubishi Trading Company, has baldly appealed to racial feelings, invoking the stale shibboleths of the past. "Now is the right time for us colored Asian races to unite again," he says. Also: "I believe the concept of the prewar Greater East-Asia Co-prosperity Sphere was right. We must look to the interests of just our own country." If a contradiction lies within this last sentence, it is blithely overlooked.

One way to help build a big navy is to spend more money on oceanological research, especially in the seas around Japan. Keidanren has been pushing such research since the late 1960's. Already, the government has conducted major research in the Malacca Strait, sending its own scientists and ships. Japan's navy—officially, the Maritime Self-Defense Forces—has actually held sea exercises in the vicinity of the Malacca Strait.

Japan's shipbuilders, who lead the world in tonnage of ships launched each year, look to the nation as a large and dependable customer for the 1970's and 1980's. Total naval tonnage under the fourth build-up program is twice the former plan—or about 20,000 tons a year. Warship construction takes longer and is far more expensive than the building of merchant vessels. Japan's naval plans call for a modern fleet of warships by 1980 that will include helicopter carriers, a missile cruiser, missile frigates, destroyers, and submarines.

Since no nation presents a real threat to Japanese shores, the reason for a big naval build-up must be sought elsewhere. The zaikai think in terms of economic development and of military gaps. They wish to fill the gap—sometimes called a vacuum—left by the withdrawal of British forces from Southeast Asia as well as the gradual decline of U.S. military power in the Western Pacific. Yoichiro Makita, president of MHI until his death in 1971, said that Japan must shoulder part of the American defense burden in the Orient.

It was the basic policy of General MacArthur's headquarters to dissolve the zaibatsu because of their role in helping to force militarism on Japan. But the zaibatsu are now fatter than in prewar days, with the industrial giants revolving around big banks such as Fuji, Mitsubishi, Mitsui, Sumitomo, Dai-Ichi Kangyo, and Sanwa. Perhaps the key difference between prewar and postwar zaibatsu is their leadership. Formerly, the huge monopolies were run by families; now there is more of a republican atmosphere. But the all-out drive for newer and bigger markets is still there. Moreover, the links with the military are expanding.

The Defense Agency made two important announcements in 1971 with far-reaching consequences for big business and the nation. First, it informally asked industry to employ ten thousand military men separated from service each year. This would establish a kind of technological exchange system between military and industry. Second, the Agency told industry it would advance by at least six months some $500 million in defense equipment payments in order to stimulate business activity. Such a sum is a vitalizing factor for any thriving economy. These moves showed graphically how smoothly industry and the military can complement each other.

Industry also took steps which would, in effect, make the military a firm pillar of the nation's economy. Here are some examples:

The Defense Agency and Keidanren started regular

monthly meetings in 1970 to promote the defense industry.

Industry agreed to put more emphasis on technological research and development in making armaments. This "R and D" program involves huge sums of government money and is an enticement to a growing defense industry.

Government and industry agreed in principle to a boosting of Japan's defense in proportion to rising national wealth.

Industry, it appears, even anticipated the Defense Agency's plan to get large companies to hire military men released from service. In 1969, the official in charge of Keidanren's Defense Production Committee, Tetsuya Senga, said industry wanted to employ all men who had received technical training for at least three years in the Self-Defense Forces (SDF). This, incidentally, would help make recruiting for the Self-Defense Forces easier.

Senga, who later became managing director of Keidanren, said: "The SDF are called unproductive, so we want to help them become productive." He also suggested a formula whereby trained technicians in industry would work for Defense Agency research organs on temporary duty and, upon completion of such work, would return to their regular jobs. More importantly, he said leaders of big business should serve as Director-General of the Defense Agency, a Cabinet post.

Such proposals naturally add fuel to charges, both at home and abroad, of a growing military-industrial complex. Senga himself realized this, for he said of his proposals: "The trouble is they may be criticized as contributing to a Japanese military-industrial complex."

Japan's military personnel has already gained a foothold in industry. Tomoharu Nishimura, former Chief of Staff of the Maritime Self-Defense Forces, is adviser to Kawasaki

Heavy Industries, which is part of the zaibatsu. In 1966—as Rear Admiral Nishimura—he was an outspoken advocate of a big navy to protect Japan's life lines, which extended all the way from Japan to the Indian Ocean. Since joining Kawasaki, Nishimura has called for a tripling of the military forces, giving emphasis to naval build-up. His call for build-up will actually be realized by 1981, when Japan's navy will have virtually tripled in size. It will go up to at least 320,000 tons.

The military-industry links in Japan are not yet like the American model where, in 1970, over two thousand retired officers of the rank of colonel and higher were holding top jobs in U.S. defense industries. But Japan is going in the same direction, if by slow motion. Between 1960 and 1970, approximately 420 Japanese generals and admirals, and hundreds of other high-echelon officers were given executive jobs in Japan's defense industries after they retired. Mitsubishi Heavy Industries, for example, has a number of prominent retired military men on its staff. They include Ichiro Sugita, former Chief of Staff of the Ground Self-Defense Forces, and Mitsugi Ihara, former Chief of Staff of the Maritime Self-Defense Forces.

Another way industry and military have joined hands is the unique plan whereby industry sends young male employees to Self-Defense Force training camps for short periods. Japanese firms have been doing this for a decade or longer. Business leaders say the discipline at these camps makes the young men better and more loyal workers. Strangely, the young men are uncomplaining. Some company officials say they prefer to hire men who have already undergone this military training. Obviously, men who learn to take orders without question from superiors are unlikely to join in left-wing demonstrations or otherwise disrupt company affairs.

The zaibatsu have a record of teaming up with militarists to enlarge Japanese territory and build up superior armed forces. General MacArthur's headquarters reported that the zaibatsu had given cash, stocks, and property to Premier-General Tojo. Conquest and plunder helped to fuel industrial machines. Overseas adventures were often rationalized by patriotic and nationalistic slogans. Generals and admirals were often linked to the zaibatsu and to political circles. Between the zaibatsu and the politicians there were important marriages, both figuratively and literally. This is still true today.

But not all militarists approved of the zaibatsu. Many young and idealistic officers who joined in plots to unseat governments in the early 1930's were anticapitalist and regarded zaibatsu leaders and the ruling circles as responsible for national ills, especially the plight of farmers and small communities. Many of these officers came from such communities. Their slogans combined anti-industrialism, anti-urbanism, and antimodernism. In 1932, ultranationalists killed Baron Takuma Dan, a Mitsui zaibatsu director, and also Finance Minister Junnosuke Inouye. The murders were carried out by the Blood Pledge Corps, a group that included agrarian fanatics and that had many supporters among the military. A similarity exists in other countries, where radical officers, mostly from the lower middle classes, have sometimes revolted against the government. This is true in Egypt and in various Latin American nations.

Can Japan's defense expenditure take up some of the slack in the economy if there is a lull in business, or if the market for a certain product falls off? The answer seems to be yes.

If a firm has a business slump, it may be able to switch to munitions making with a minimum amount of change. Some Japanese firms, finding it tough to market textiles or tableware, have asked for the help of the Defense Agency —and have received it. The Agency, under its build-up plan, stresses domestic production of munitions—everything from jet engines to missiles. If costs must be cut, they are often in the purchases to be made of foreign weapons.

In 1971 a metal-tableware manufacturer in Tsubame City, northwest of Tokyo, said it wished to enter the munitions business in order to tide it over the prevailing business recession due to a falling off of exports to the United States. The firm said it could make excellent interior parts for airplanes and also military radio equipment. Reportedly, the firm received a contract from the Defense Agency. Since the defense industry is viewed as a growth stock, it was unlikely the Tsubame firm would ever go back to making knives and forks. Howa Industry Corporation also started its life as a maker of textile equipment. Now it is Japan's ace rifle manufacturer.

As befits its role in an economic superpower, the Defense Agency is not stingy. Before long, Japan may have the world's most expensive tank. One unit alone would cost $630,000. This price is said to be one-fifth higher than that of the British Centurion tank, and it is far higher than that of German, French, and Swedish models. Nippon Steel, the world's largest steel maker, has been asked to provide the steel for the tank, and Mitsubishi Electric and Nippon Electric will probably provide the electronics for about six hundred of the elite tanks, planned for completion during the fifth defense build-up.

A comparable tank would have been the projected U.S.-German dream tank, a joint Main Battle Tank—called MBT-70—whose cost threatened to climb to $750,000 each, or twice the early estimate. The tank, with gun-missile weapons systems and other new features, came under the review of the Nixon Administration, which rejected it as too costly and problematical. Meanwhile, the Germans had dropped out of the joint effort, presumably because of spiraling costs. Instead, a new American futuristic tank is planned, to cost a maximum of $415,000. Though high, it is much under the estimate for the new Japanese tank.

The cost of making a Phantom jet fighter bomber is reported to be about $5.5 million—or six times more than that of the F-104 Starfighter, the former mainstay airplane for Japan's Air Self-Defense Force. If the Phantom were bought directly from America, the cost would be half as much, it is said. But the Defense Agency is willing to spend about $2.75 million per plane extra to have Mitsubishi Heavy Industries build them under American license. The reason? Japan thereby equips itself with the latest production techniques and facilities for a very modern warplane. Mitsubishi was scheduled to build about two hundred Phantom jets during the mid-1970's.

By 1976, Japan will have risen from approximately twelfth place in the world to sixth or seventh, in military spending. Ahead of Japan will be only the United States, Russia, China, West Germany, France, and perhaps Britain. Even this growth is regarded as too small by various Japanese industrial leaders.

A key point, as we have seen, is that Japan's military expenses, while still behind that of the major powers of Western Europe, do not include the most costly weapons

of all—nuclear weapons, heavy bombers, and aircraft carriers. Some military analysts say that this deficiency will
disappear in due time.

There are some links between the Japanese and American defense industries. Sometimes the Pentagon acts as
intermediary. On a visit to Japan in July 1971, U.S. Defense Secretary Laird said America hoped for close cooperation between both nations' munitions industries. In the
same year, the Defense Department joined with the Defense Orientation Conference Association, a group of leading U.S. munitions makers, to invite twenty-one members
of the Japanese Defense Society to the United States for a
two-week tour of military bases. The visitors included the
president of Mitsubishi Heavy Industries, the presidents
or managing directors of other zaibatsu, and Tetsuya Senga
of Keidanren. Two years previously, a U.S. mission com-
prised of twenty-five presidents of munitions firms had
visited Japan.

Three months after the Laird visit, Japan said it was prepared to buy up to $1 billion worth of American weapons
during the fourth defense program. Japan bought about
$500 million under the third defense plan.

Although Japan's military-industrial complex is not in
the same class as the American supermodel, a few captains
of industry in Japan are beginning to worry about the
direction of their economy. Yoshizane Iwasa, chairman of
the board of Fuji Bank, one of Japan's biggest banks, and
a part of the zaibatsu, gave this warning in an article in
Pacific Community, in April 1970: "What requires constant watchfulness is the tendency for increases in military
spending to become self-propelling. Appropriate safeguards
must be applied to nip in the bud even the slightest tendency to build a system resembling the prewar militarism."

Iwasa, who often leads economic missions overseas, spoke of the undesirability of a Japanese military-industrial complex that might emerge. He said such a complex might be caused by expansion of the munitions industry. Iwasa also said: "The strategic conceptions underlying arguments for adopting nuclear weapons favor ascendancy of the military, and thus entail no small danger of a resurgence of militarism."

One year later, Yoshitaro Inayama, president of Nippon Steel Corporation, which now outproduces the United States Steel Corporation, told me that there were strong voices among the zaikai calling for Japan to go nuclear so Japan would not be used as a whipping boy by the other economic powers.

American experts on Japan have begun to take notice of the Japanese military-industrial complex. George W. Ball, a financier and former Undersecretary of State, said in testimony before Congress in November 1971:

In spite of the loose talk in the United States about something called a military-industrial complex, the structure of Japanese institutions is ideally designed for such a development. . . . In fact, there are already reports of pressures in the industrial sector of Japan for the domestic construction of sophisticated armaments.

Hanson W. Baldwin, the retired military analyst of *The New York Times,* commented in 1970:

The industrial-military complex does not run modern Japan, but it is part of the establishment, and the industrial part of it—highly influential in both economics and politics—is demonstrating an increasing interest in, and capability for, the manufacture of armaments.

For some years, Japan was not officially in the arms-export business. Even at present there is much sensitivity to such epithets as merchants of death and war industries, and to the claim made by some critics that Japan will become Asia's arsenal sooner or later.

The government says weapons may be exported only if they are weapons for defense. But the sale of weapons has been banned in three areas: Communist nations, nations involved in conflicts, and nations to which a United Nations resolution has prohibited arms sales. These principles have not been rigidly followed, and early in the 1970's the Japan Weapons Industry Association was raising its voice, asking the government to relax its three principles.

However, the public still opposes with zeal any sale of military equipment overseas. By resort to euphemism, Japan has been able to avoid the glare of publicity on sales of various small arms abroad. Shipments of rifles and pistols for the Thai police forces have been labeled "hunting equipment." Small consignments of arms to nations such as Singapore and Malaya have had the word "samples" stamped on the shipping crates.

If left-wing opposition parties had got wind of what was really inside the crates, the revelations would have put the government in an awkward and embarrassing position.

About the year 1959, the Saigon government asked whether Japan could put up an ammunitions plant near the capital. A Japanese munitions firm which was then producing 30 million bullets and tracer shells a year and enjoying a special procurement boom from sales to American military forces, accepted South Vietnam's request, and in due course the munitions maker shipped a whole bullet-making plant. The crates were labeled "machine tools." Industrial sources said the "tools" were hardly checked by government inspectors before shipment, despite the three principles for arms exports, one of which forbade sales of weapons to countries at war.

Such a ruse does not appear to be exceptional. In 1967, Japan gave the Philippines, as part of war reparations, an ammunition plant worth $5 million, with an annual capacity of 15 million rounds. The shipment, sent in secrecy, was labeled "metal processing machinery." But this arms export was so successful that a Japanese bullet manufacturer later hired a leading public relations firm to make a motion picture in color explaining bullet-making machines to the Filipinos. There was some Japanese protest, but not much. One labor union carried out a one-hour strike against the film, coupling opposition to the film with demands for a pay increase. Yet the union's protest was a serious one. The union said: "This is not simply a publicity film, but it provides a springboard for the exporting of Japan-made weapons to Southeast Asia."

A sale of military equipment to Sweden, a country at peace, was publicly announced in 1971, when Kawasaki Heavy Industries agreed to sell Sweden some antisubmarine helicopters by the end of 1974. There were some perfunctory protests by opposition parties. It is said that Japan has received requests for munitions, including aircraft and warships, from nearly every country which is not at peace either with itself or with its neighbors and which is unable to make those weapons itself. Military sources say such requests have come from states involved in the Middle East imbroglio, but they have gone unfulfilled. Japan is most discreet in such matters, since it has relations with most countries of the world.

Surpluses of arms may be exported, says the Japanese government, but all such sales must be handled on a case-by-case basis. The United States, a close ally, takes it for granted that Japan will become a prime exporter of arms to non-Communist Asian nations to equip their armies. U.S. diplomat-financier Eugene R. Black said such arms sales could be rationalized in Japan as simply a good commercial proposition. Black, former president of the World Bank added: "I would not rule out such a development as being in the U.S. interest."

Minoru Yamada, vice president of Daikin Kogyo, a manufacturing company, is frank on the subject of arms-making. He says: "We were called merchants of death for making ordnance for the Americans in the Korean War, but we had no other way for rebirth except by being merchants of death."

In short, Japan's weapons industry, which was knocked to pieces by defeat in war, was restored to life by another war. It has been said that the economy of modern Japan fattened on successive wars, beginning with the Sino-Japanese War of 1894–95, and proceeding through the Russo-Japanese War, World War I, the Manchuria Incident, and the second Sino-Japanese War. The Pacific War was an exception.

There is one school of thought which holds that an index to whether or not Japan becomes fully militarized is the extent of weapons exports. Whatever the merit of this theory, given the present flux in Southeast Asia, Japan is certain to receive many requests for arms in the future.

Already the list of those nations importing Japan-made "bombs, grenades, and similar munitions of war"—the wording is taken from an official list of Japanese exports—is expanding. In 1971, Taiwan, South Korea, and the Philippines were buying such Japanese small arms as pistols and revolvers. Interestingly, South Africa, New

Zealand, the United States, France, and Peru were included on the list of those buying small amounts of Japanese weapons. The quantity of arms sold was not in itself significant: only 86 tons. But like most Japanese exports, this one, too, seems destined to rise.*

---

* Interestingly, Japanese-made American Armalite high velocity rifles, which can fire 40 bullets per minute, found their way into Northern Ireland. In May 1972 reports from Belfast said that Irish Republican Army gunmen had begun to use these Japanese arms, although Japanese makers of these rifles denied they had exported them to Ireland.

3

The New Military

War is the father of creation and the mother of culture.

> —From "Basic Principles of National Defense and Proposal for Defense Build-up" (1934)

Militarism is a ghost that we must always watch carefully.

> —Zentaro Kosaka, postwar foreign minister, from interview in 1970 with *Mainichi* newspapers

Most Japanese people believe their country must be defended in emergency, but they do not completely trust those whose duty it is to defend it. Vivid memories of the recent past account for much of the suspicion toward the military. Moreover, there is a deep sensitivity among the people about contemporary military matters, and various polls show many citizens feel militarism is either being revived or such a possibility exists in the future.

The image the Self-Defense Forces wish to convey is that of a peaceful and democratic military, which is the same image most nations' military forces wish to convey. The SDF looks very different from the defunct Imperial forces. All, or nearly all, of the face slapping is gone, as well as other harsh disciplinary practices. Even the uniforms look more democratic, or at any rate, more plebeian.

Yet, when one visits SDF bases, one is sometimes startled to see a display or two that invoke the blood and iron of the war years. At the navy's officer-training school at Etajima, near Hiroshima, are preserved mementos of youthful kamikaze suicide pilots who went on one-way missions against the enemy. Among the memorabilia is a blood-stained letter of a young officer who lost his life. Battle flags and photographs of the heroic pilots are exhibited.

Of course, such keepsakes help promote a fondness for the wartime exploits, and they also foster patriotic feelings which were suppressed at the war's end as part of the democratic reforms. Seeing such reminders of the nation's vio-

lent past, one or two officer candidates at the school decided to quit on the spot and return to civilian life.

The people's anxiety is not quieted by the government's
loose interpretation of the Constitution. For instance, the
government has declared that it is perfectly legal for Japan
to possess small, tactical nuclear weapons; that, in emergency, Japan may send the Self-Defense Forces abroad; and
that, in fact, all weapons and armaments are permitted, as
long as they are for defensive and not offensive purposes.

The government often said that it was a basic principle
not to allow nuclear weapons to be brought into Japan.
But every time a U.S. nuclear-powered submarine or other
modern warship entered a Japanese port, many citizens
felt unusually nervous. While innocently expecting that
American warships would not have the dreaded weapons
on board when they came into port cities, the public was
not absolutely sure. Then, in 1971, *The New York Times*
reported what many Japanese had suspected: U.S. warships
were in fact coming into Japan with nuclear weapons on
board. The disclosure served to shatter any existing illu-
sions about these shipboard weapons among the Japanese
public.

Conscription, which is anathema to the public because
it is so closely associated with militarization, has been given
priority in many hypothetical war plans compiled solely
by the Self-Defense Forces or sometimes jointly with
American forces. Lists of eligible young men and a com-
puterized number system for the entire population are
being prepared; both would help very nicely if and when
conscription is adopted.

Almost every man in the 180,000-strong Ground Self-
Defense Forces, which has turned into a quite respectable
army, has the training and ability to be a noncommissioned

officer or of officer rank. This army is producing a surplus of NCO's. In other words, if the military were to be doubled or tripled, there would be no shortage of officers and NCO's. A perceptive Australian journalist, Murray Sayle, has noted that the Treaty of Versailles allowed the Weimar Republic only a 100,000-man army. At present, the West German Army has approximately 326,000 men, the British Army has 168,000, and the French 328,000. Although these numerical strengths vary from year to year, the reader will observe that Japan has a slightly larger army than Britain.

One hypothetical war plan, called Three Arrows, was drafted by fifty-three staff officers, 90 per cent of whom were graduates of the defunct Imperial Military Academy. This plan, drawn up in the early 1960's for use in a war situation on the Korean peninsula, bore the surprising notation that the wartime Tojo regime's "Basic Principles for the Empire's National Policies" would "provide good introductory remarks." These jingoistic "Basic Principles" were appended to the plan.

Many Japanese feel the nation's defense forces have actually passed beyond the limits of self-defense and therefore could become involved in other nations' problems. Whether or not such fears may be dismissed as silly, the government has in fact laid the groundwork for such use of its forces. And in 1971 the Defense Agency even made the curious proposal that the Self-Defense Forces be sent overseas as part of natural disaster and relief teams.

There is apprehension over the fact that Japan extended its Air Defense Identification Zone (ADIZ) to encompass the Senkaku Islands. These islands are claimed by Japan, China, and Taiwan. The ADIZ means Japanese fighter planes can scramble whenever an unidentified plane enters the zone. Peking went so far as to call Japan's claim to the islands the first step taken by Japanese militarism openly to conquer territory in Asia. Although such a charge seems farfetched, many observers felt that the Japanese air-defense move was provocative.

Professor Yoshikazu Sakamoto, an international law expert at prestigious Tokyo University, says one of the most dangerous trends in Japan's defense policy is expansion of the nation's defense zone in accordance with enlarged military capacity. That expanding defense policy is being established without prior national consensus on the basic principles of national security.

Riot-control training by the Self-Defense Forces has been stepped up in recent years. A man who was formerly director-general of the Defense Agency, Munenori Akagi, has envisaged this possibility: "If the SDF are mobilized, they will carry arms. Then, it may happen that the soldiers, enraged at abusive words heaped on them by the demonstrators, will open fire, leading to a horrible carnage."

It was Akagi, among others, who counseled the government not to use the Self-Defense Forces in 1960 to help quell the massive demonstrations against the revision of the U.S.-Japan security treaty. The SDF was not used, and Japan had to cancel the visit by President Eisenhower, whose entourage had actually come as close as Okinawa.

An SDF paratroop officer was once asked how he would react in an emergency riot situation. His reply was enlightening: "The question of whether or not we will point our guns at our own people when mobilized to maintain peace and order is too sentimental. Once we are ordered into action, we will not retreat."

Another SDF officer, of higher rank, made this remarkable statement:

A much greater prudence is required in Japan for mobilizing the SDF for police action than in America which is formed by many ethnic groups. . . . In the United States the National Guard and Army troops on active duty can be called out for police action comparatively easily, and these troops fire on hostile crowds with little inhibition. In Japan, the troops would be firing at people who are compatriots in the strictly racial sense of the word.

These statements, quoted in the respected *Mainichi* newspapers, were made before the killing of four students and the wounding of nine others by U.S. National Guardsmen at Kent State University, Ohio, in 1970.*

It is of singular interest to contrast these feelings with remarks made by Chou En-lai describing how Chinese soldiers are taught to restrain their anger. Chou's words were quoted by Aiichiro Fujiyama, a ruling party lawmaker who met him in Peking in 1971. Chou said:

We attach special importance to political education of the military. We teach the Army not to become angry at the general masses, not to talk back even when the soldiers are abused by the people, not to hit back when they are hit by the people, and not to shoot at the people, even if the people try to take away their rifles. This is what Chairman Mao teaches and it is by this that the Army has the trust of the general masses of the people.

Many new Japanese military officers are too young to have served in World War II. But the links between the Defense Agency and officers of the former Imperial Army or Imperial Navy are strong and meaningful. In 1966 the

---

* And before British soldiers killed thirteen Irish Catholics in a Londonderry demonstration in January 1972.

Agency drew up a plan to mobilize one hundred retired generals as defense advisers in order to organize a big reserve force of 320,000 ex-SDF men. Most of these generals had served in the Imperial forces.

Numerous plans for reserve forces have already been drawn up. One plan, compiled by a Cabinet official, calls for setting up a million-man militia. Another urges formation of a 60,000-man guard corps, with units in every prefecture, to be modeled after the U.S. National Guard.

The influence of former Imperial officers on the Self-Defense Forces appears to be deep and abiding. These officers, middle-aged or older, as well as politicians of the same generation, show a natural tendency to justify and rationalize the Pacific War and their roles in it, although veterans as well as intellectuals in Japan and other countries, too, have thoughtfully re-examined, reinterpreted, and sometimes criticized their own nations' roles in the war.

Retired General Minoru Genda, who helped plan the Pearl Harbor attack and was later Chief of Staff of the Air Self-Defense Force, says his only regret was that Japan did not bomb Pearl Harbor enough. Also, if Japan had had the atomic bomb it would have used it, he says. Genda, a member of the National Diet, made similar statements during a lecture tour of America a few years ago. A few Americans were embittered, but Genda received U.S. military honors.

Here is the approximate distribution of ex-Imperial officers in the Self-Defense Forces (as of 1970):

80 per cent of the colonels and generals in the Ground Self-Defense Force

90 per cent of the captains and admirals in the Maritime Self-Defense Force

70 per cent of the top-ranking officers in the Air Self-Defense Force

The military build-up plans for the 1970's and 1980's call for emphasis on a big navy. At the present time, however, Japan is already the leading naval power in Asia, excluding the U.S. and Soviet fleets. China says it is forsaking superpower status. But Japan is not. The hawks in the ruling party and within the SDF often state such ideas frankly, if unofficially.

The Defense Agency's goal is a navy of 300,000 to 350,000 tons by 1980, a minimum of thirteen divisions for the ground forces, and an air force of 1,200 planes. The one or two helicopter carriers, which will join the Japanese fleet around 1975, are said to be a substitute for a long-smoldering dream within the agency to build a 30,000-ton attack carrier. But some experts say that such an impossible dream may not be impossible for Japan in the years ahead.

At the beginning of 1972, Japan had approximately 130,000 tons of warships, about 920 aircraft, and 180,000 soldiers, in addition to a 36,000-man reserve force. Japan had nearly thirty destroyers, half that many frigates, and ten submarines. Most of these ships were new, built in Japanese shipyards, and some were equipped with the latest conventional missiles. The Defense Agency has plans to add nuclear-driven submarines to the fleet, probably around 1980.

By comparison, China has around thirty submarines, all diesel-powered, plus two dozen or so destroyers and escorts, and an assortment of smaller, coastal craft. China is building several nuclear submarines, according to the authoritative *Jane's Fighting Ships*.

Almost each year for over a decade, Japan has sent a

flotilla of destroyers, sometimes including submarines, all
over the world as training fleets. Such fleets have steamed
into Pearl Harbor, the English Channel, and the Malacca
Strait to hold exercises. This is a record equaled only by
the United States.

Japanese rearmament calls for an additional twenty
RF-4E reconnaissance planes before 1976. Defense Agency
officials say these high-flying intelligence-gathering aircraft
are needed to meet the projected pullout of American air
power from Japan. The basic purpose of the RF-4E is to
photograph enemy terrain, as well as to take radar pictures.

This plane, styled after the well-known Phantom jet
fighter-bomber, can fly at nearly twice the speed of sound.
Its combat range is about a thousand miles. If based on
Okinawa, its range covers a large part of coastal China.
Or, if based in northern Japan, it can reach the Soviet
maritime provinces and offshore islands. If flown from
South Korea, the plane can fly to Peking and back.

In addition, the Defense Agency will have a half dozen
or so refueling planes to enable jet fighters such as the
Phantom to extend their flying time, despite the fact that
Japan is so narrow that such planes can cross its width in
less than ten minutes. Such fast and powerful warplanes,
which can carry nuclear bombs, make the Chinese wary.

It is being said that a major reason for the increased
Japanese military build-up, and the addition of new missiles for warships and planes, is to cope with reductions in
U.S. bases and reductions in the Seventh Fleet. But it is
clear that if Japan builds up its military forces, always
using the withdrawals of U.S. forces from Japan and other
parts of Asia as a pretext, then Japan will in time possess
a vast fighting machine.

Some Japanese commentators say the cost of the sixth build-up plan (1982–86) will be triple that of the fourth, and that it makes allowance for nuclear weapons. The Defense Agency has already compiled unofficial studies concerning arming the Self-Defense Forces with nuclear missiles, including a seaborne antiballistic-missile (ABM) fleet.

Popular misgivings about military matters stem in part from a legacy of military meddling in politics. There is no long tradition of civilian control over the nation's military forces. Although the head of the Defense Agency is a civilian, chosen by the Prime Minister, he usually remains in his post for one year only, scarcely time enough for him to visit all the military bases and shake hands with his top officers.

The rebelliousness of the military during the 1930's is vividly remembered by many citizens. Hardly a year passed when the nation was not convulsed by one or more antigovernment plots masterminded by ultranationalists and militarists, including many young officers. Eventually, the fanatics got what they wanted: an all-out military regime. However, those officers who opposed the zaibatsu and the political clique which ran the country could hardly rejoice; the succeeding military governments entered into a close partnership with the industrialists and the old civil bureaucracy.

The following are among the best-known episodes of that bygone era:

1931: March Incident; an attempt by army officers and civilian extremists to seize control of the National Diet and establish a military regime for the purpose of expansion overseas.

1931: October Incident; similar to the former one, and some

of the same officers were involved, but much more violence was plotted. The ringleaders planned to assassinate the entire Cabinet by aerial bombardment and had gathered bombs for this purpose.

1932: May 15 Incident; young naval officers, with support from civilian ultranationalists, failed in a coup attempt but fatally shot Prime Minister Takeshi Inukai.

1933: Shimpeitai Incident; ultranationalist officers of the Heaven-Sent Soldiers' Corps plotted to kill top political and business leaders but were foiled in advance by police.

1934: November Incident; Tokyo War College students planned to assassinate the Prime Minister, a cautious moderate, and other high officials. The ringleaders were caught and merely suspended from active duty.

1936: February 26 Incident; the best-known of all the incidents. About two dozen young officers, imbued with the radical ideas of Ikki Kita, the ultranationalist fanatic, led a revolt of more than one thousand soldiers. They killed the Lord Keeper of the Privy Seal, who was a former Prime Minister; the Finance Minister; the military education inspector; and a colonel who was mistaken for the Prime Minister. Thirteen army officers and four civilians (including Ikki Kita) were tried and executed, to the surprise of many. Hitherto, many plotters had become almost national heroes, and were jailed briefly, or set free.

After the 1936 incident, the most militaristic and ultranationalistic elements among military men and civilians joined hands to steer the country on its calamitous path to defeat.

A few attempts to foment a *coup d'état* in the postwar years have made citizens nervous. One of them is the Sanmu Incident of 1961, in which thirteen extreme nationalists, some of them former Imperial officers, planned to kill the Prime Minister and his Cabinet and take over the National Diet in order to "save the nation from a Leftist plot." Police confiscated hand grenades, rifles, and other weapons. One of the ringleaders arrested was Taku Mikami, who was arrested and jailed in the bloody May 15 Incident of 1932, when he was a young navy lieutenant. In addition, the Mishima Incident of 1970 was, in actuality, a frustrated attempt to incite a rebellion among members of the Self-Defense Forces.

Was the secret hypothetical war plan, *Mitsuya* (Three Arrows), drafted by top-echelon SDF officers in the 1960's, a rehearsal plan for a military takeover of the government? The plan was leaked to the Socialist Party, and that is what they claimed. The plan envisaged full-fledged wartime mobilization, including censorship of the mass media, and controls over the Diet and the economy. This, said the Socialists, was similar to the February 26 Incident, in which military officers sought a complete military takeover of national affairs. Top goverment officials admitted the plan was drawn up without the knowledge of civilian authorities, even within the SDF. So the Socialists, and other critics, could not be accused of mere squeamishness.

Since there is only a short tradition of democracy in the postwar era, many civilians feel the best antidote to a military comeback is to hold the military forces to as small a size as possible, making sure the aims, plans, and weapons of these forces are of a defensive nature. But, of course, each additional build-up by the military, like the acquisition of napalm and Phantom jets, has been justified in the name of defense.

Is the SDF legal? The problem continues to frustrate military men, for they are taught to die willingly for their country whose Constitution denies their very existence. The men under arms are often praised by the government and civilian leaders, who say SDF men are the "most patriotic Japanese," deserving special honor and respect for their job of defending the country against the smallest sign of external threat. According to many SDF officers and men, the citizens are insufficiently grateful.

The citizens, however, are caught in a dilemma. They wish to honor the Self-Defense Forces, but they also have vivid recollections of chauvinistic and arrogant men in uniform. Many can still remember when soldiers demanded, and got, seats on crowded buses and trains, and in every way were first in the community. Since ordinary civilians suffered from militarism, the idea lingers that having an army, however small, is risky.

Professor Tsuyoshi Manabe, a constitutional-law expert at Saga University in Kyushu, says 90 per cent of the nation's specialists on the Constitution view the SDF as illegal. The problem has never been finally settled by the courts, although they have generally taken a position in support of the SRF's right to exist.

The birth of the Self-Defense Forces was clothed in secrecy. Because the public opposed the rise of a full-fledged armed force so soon after the most destructive and miserable war in Japan's history (which was blamed on the militarists), the Government acted clandestinely. But even if the Constitution was changed, with a clause inserted saying that armed forces may exist, the debate goes on; some suspicion will probably always linger that the nation's postwar military force was an illegitimate child. As one industrialist waggishly expressed it: "The baby was born despite the 'no, no.' "

The new officer corps came from the ranks of the purged, the many thousands whose careers had abruptly halted with Japan's defeat. Many were jobless and were glad to wear a uniform again and receive regular paychecks. Before being allowed to command troops, they were first given an orientation course in democracy, to put them in step with the new Japan. It was supposed to be a new military force without the excesses that marked the old. But since many of the same militarists who had served during World War II, were back in uniform, the public, which is usually wise in such matters, was alarmed. Given such a background, one might safely predict that the officers would never be content to maintain a puny military force but would wish to build a strong army, navy, and air force.

Shortly after Japan's postwar military forces were born in the early 1950's various grandiose plans were proposed for future growth. One was the Hattori Plan of Colonel Takushiro Hattori. He was personal adviser on military affairs to Prime Minister Shigeru Yoshida. Reinstated Hattori had been secretary to General Hideki Tojo and was a member of the general staff's operations division. After the war ended, he was put in charge of demobilization and got to know the home addresses of many important ex-officers. His plan called for a build-up to 300,000 men on the ground, 300,000 tons of warships for the navy, and 3,000 planes for the air force. It was just a plan, similar to others put forward in the early 1950's, and it was not implemented.

In 1952, a government committee drew up a long-range defense plan, listing the build-up Japan needed for independent defense. It called for:

Ground forces: 1 million men
Navy: 1.5 million tons
Aircraft: 10,000 planes

The armament listed was worthy of an aspiring super-power.

Seventeen years later—in 1969—the Defense Agency put together a plan for autonomous defense based on the twin premises that the U.S.-Japan security pact had been abolished and that a new Constitution was functioning. The highlight of this plan was that Japan should independently develop and possess nuclear weapons and the intercontinental ballistic missiles to deliver such weapons. This was to be Japan's deterrent power.

Furthermore, the plan required two and possibly three naval task forces, with each task force to consist of one attack carrier, one missile cruiser, and three to four destroyers. In addition, it outlined a conscription system and universal military training for all men. The thirteen existing army divisions were to be increased to approximately twenty. Finally, to cope with invasion, the plan stated that Japan needed heavy bombers capable of carrying nuclear bombs. The plan said several squadrons of such bombers, with twenty-five of these planes in each squadron, were desirable.

The notes accompanying this extraordinary plan were of considerable interest. They said large sums of money were needed to develop and manufacture nuclear weapons. France, it was pointed out, spent more than $5.6 billion to produce atomic weapons, plus more than $2.5 billion for bombers, missiles, and submarines as a delivery system. The notes also pointed out that if Japan was to have an independent defense, it must allocate at least $5.5 billion each year for military purposes—roughly the amount spent annually by the major Western European powers.*

---

* Yet for all the billions of francs the French have spent developing their *force de frappe,* they do not appear to have either effective self-produced

A curious note: the amount cited in the 1969 Defense Agency plan as a necessary expenditure for this huge build-up is roughly equal to the estimated yearly budget for Japan's fifth defense build-up, which begins in 1977.

Learning the contents of the plan, the opposition parties fired away at the government, which proffered the lame explanation that the plan was prepared at the request of "a certain ruling party lawmaker for his study."

How big can the SDF actually grow? The question is hard to answer with certainty. But one must always bear in mind that, as an economic superpower, Japan has all the resources in money and material to field a vast military force. Japan does not suffer from the financial pinch of many other advanced countries.

Nevertheless, though Japan surely has the wealth to put together a much bigger military, with nuclear arms, many liberal economists and scholars are chagrined that the question can even arise when, for example, the spending on public works has been so scanty. Thus, a third of the private homes in the capital city are still without flush toilets. According to official statistics, the sewage system covers only 40 per cent of Tokyo.

The SDF can rather easily rise to the hopes of the Hattori Plan. Such a build-up depends very much on the following three conditions: (1) whether a keen rivalry with China will arise; (2) whether an American pullout from Asia, including reduction of U.S. bases in Japan and South Korea, comes about, and the Japanese government, with at least partial support, deems it vital to compensate for this withdrawal by its own military increase; and (3)

---

nuclear weapons or delivery systems. Needless to say, the amount the SDF would allocate here is just a drop in the ocean compared to the total United States and Soviet development costs.

whether an economic slowdown occurs so that the government decides to sink some of its huge financial savings into full-scale militarization.

To offset the people's fears concerning the current steady military build-up, the Defense Agency is carrying out various public-relations campaigns, some of them with particular gusto. For many years, SDF men have helped in time of natural disasters, such as those caused by typhoons; they have aided in snow removal or helped in the Olympic Games; they have also helped apple growers and rice planters.

On occasion, Defense Agency public-relations efforts were so good that the U.S. Defense Department, which is hard to beat in this field, took notice. For example, one SDF film about Japan's defense was promptly bought by the Pentagon. Another film cunningly had the appearance of a science film. It showed a test firing of an American ICBM, but it also showed actual scenes of the Big E, or the nuclear aircraft carrier *Enterprise,* on combat duty in the Gulf of Tonkin, with jet planes being launched against the enemy. This film's original title had to do with the U.S.-Japan security system. But before it was shown to the public, the name was changed by shrewd distributors to *Wonders of Science.*

Japan has long been a master in making use of the mass media and the educational system to indoctrinate the public. Professor Reischauer has noted that Japan was decades ahead of Germany in perfecting its skills in controlling its citizens.

Sports, predominantly the martial arts, are another means the SDF uses to promote itself, as well as to teach youth such habits as discipline, loyalty, toughness, and combativeness. The Japanese are sports lovers, and young men are especially fond of body-contact sports: *kendo,* karate, judo, even *kempo*—the "art of the fist." Such sports are the traditional Bushido arts. The SDF runs a physical-education school that is popular with athletes and helps glamorize these sports. Many athletes enroll in this school.

Incidentally, many police and fire departments throughout Japan also encourage the Bushido arts for their young staff members. In a typical neighborhood in Tokyo, one may pass the local fire department and see a dozen young men hitting each other's padded bodies with bamboo swords while letting out blood-curdling yells in the process.

In addition to opening its physical-education school to young civilian athletes, the Defense Agency also allows thousands of young students, including high-school and primary students, to spend the summer holidays at one of its training schools near Mt. Fuji. At first, there were some perfunctory protests from parents, who labeled such a practice "militaristic." But attitudes reportedly changed when it was seen that the children, on returning home, were more obedient than before.

Each year, over five hundred pupils live for short periods at these military-school dormitories. As a result, the young students develop a liking for the military life. Girl students, too, are enrolled.

One high-school girl kept a diary of her experience at an SDF school, of which this excerpt is enlightening:

When our bus arrives at the SDF school gate, we see soldiers on guard with rifles at the ready. Are there bad people inside? I feel somewhat upset. The buildings, uniform in appearance, have a musty atmosphere. Having to spend four days in one of these buildings, I feel like the girl who wrote the *Diary of Anne Frank.* I feel so lonely that I become homesick.

But life becomes bearable, and she adds:

But how strange, while making beds with the troops, I become cheerful. The Fuji training course is an outstanding
feature of our school, after all. We follow it through to the
best of our ability so that our junior graders will follow in the
fine pattern we set for them.

In mid-1971, it was learned that six small towns in Saga
Prefecture, in Kyushu, were planning to send a total of
135 male civil employees to a nearby military base for
short periods of training. The men would be taught
spiritual culture, etiquette, and discipline. Eventually,
after vigorous protests from teachers, union leaders, and
left-wing politicians, the towns were forced to cancel these
plans. It was disclosed that such a practice is not unusual
in Japan.

The Defense Agency also sells itself to the public with
more standard public-relations activities. A typical year
(1970) shows how it promoted itself: 7,507 persons took
rides on military planes; 296,790 toured warships; 132,910
took sea cruises; 2,382,546 toured base camps; and
1,244,909 were invited to watch maneuvers. Also, the SDF
gave 5,803 concerts drawing 24,502,705 persons and there
were 24,555 showings of SDF films with 5,755,688 citizens
attending. Perhaps most important of all, 676 military
exhibitions were held in various cities throughout Japan
with 7,490,999 people attending.

As noted in the American prize-winning documentary,
The Selling of the Pentagon, produced by the Columbia
Broadcasting System, a military establishment tends to be
a "runaway bureaucracy that frustrates attempts to control it." But the irony in Japan is that the citizens' money is

being spent on public relations for a military force still under a legal shadow.

Meanwhile, SDF generals and admirals, in addition to assorted right-wing politicians and industrialists, often pillory the mass media, the leftist opposition parties, and China and the Soviet Union as well by referring to them as enemies of the people or enemies of the SDF. In this forensic battle, the SDF appears to be slightly ahead—and gaining.

4

Yukio Mishima: Culture and Fanaticism

Literary people tend to see his suicide in purely aesthetic terms, ignoring the undeniable fact that Mishima's aesthetic doctrines are inseparably linked to his political beliefs. They glorify his aesthetics, but they do not realize that in so doing they very often glorify his political causes as well. This strange combination of aesthetics and politics was widespread before the war, and became one of the strongest theoretical bases for the development of Japanese fascism and militarism.

> —Makoto Oda, author, in *The Times*, London, April 29, 1971

With the passage of time, Mishima's suicide is quietly beginning to be seen in a favorable light by members of the Self-Defense Forces.

> —Kaoru Murakami, military affairs commentator, remark made early in 1971

There are, or were, two Mishimas.

One is the stylish man of letters, often photographed in his studio with books piled high on his work desk. This is the amazingly successful author who turned out a hundred novels, plays, and other works before his death at the age of forty-five. This is the sought-after samurai poet of international society, the man with an eye cocked for the Nobel Prize, the stylist who could display charm and wit in English or Japanese. This is the man whom *Life* magazine called "a kind of god, the last emperor of the Japanese aesthetic tradition, beauty's final desperate kamikaze pilot." The words were written a few years before Mishima died.

Then there is Mishima the militaristic superpatriot who had a lust for uniforms and swords, for the martial arts and the warrior's life; who, although he lived to see the first year of the 1970's, much preferred the older and fiercer epochs in Japanese history. Here is the man who acted in gangster movies and exalted the Japanese soldier above all other citizens. He had written, "I love the Self-Defense Forces."

Mishima is the man to whom democracy meant flabbiness and femininity, as opposed to the masculinity of the martial arts; he is the man who chose as a title for one of his plays, *My Friend Hitler,* and was second to none in hating the peace Constitution; he is the man who worshiped his Emperor, who wanted to see Japan militarized, and even organized his private army, *Tate no Kai* (Society

of Shields), with a hundred young men. Mishima is said
to have spent 20 million yen (roughly $60,000) of his own
money to run this small army.

Born in 1925 as Kimitake Hiraoka, Mishima was a pale,
slight youth. At twenty he was turned down for military
service because of poor health. Like much of the rest of
the population, his mind had been filled with the glory
and patriotism of war. He was well acquainted with the
dictum of the nineteenth-century nationalist, Shoin
Yoshida, who often proclaimed: "Men of peace are dis-
loyal and unrighteous."

One can easily imagine the young Mishima's agony at
not being able to don a uniform and do battle for the
Emperor. Later, in the years just before his death, his
wardrobe was stocked with pretentious uniforms, which
he designed for himself and his Society of Shields.

Fed on such a view of war, Mishima took defeat as a
terrible humiliation. The postwar democratic reforms
were, for him a sinister influence on the people, robbing
them of their virility. Some years after World War II, he
took up body-building and soon transformed his frail
body into a ruggedly muscular physique. He was proud
of his new, rippling muscles and was often photographed
wearing only a loincloth. Sometimes he was photographed
as he exercised with a pair of dumbbells, with beads of
sweat on his face.

Because death and hara-kiri are a thread running
through Mishima's literary productions, many scholars
and writers tend to view his suicide as a kind of literary
death. He was a poet, and he was eccentric. But one cannot easily overlook the array of facts which place Mishima
in the militaristic mold.

The statue of Mishima in the Tokyo Wax Museum

depicts not a man of books but a naked warrior holding a long sword. It is just how he wished to be remembered, for he often sneered at the craft of writing. On the first anniversary of his death, after Shinto services, there were no readings from Mishima's literary works. Instead, karate and kendo were demonstrated in front of an altar prepared on the stage.

In one of his suicide notes, Mishima said he wanted a life-size bronze statue of himself erected at a place where Mt. Fuji and the sea can be seen. His family has had a life-size nude statue of Mishima made by a Tokyo sculptor.

The Self-Defense Forces viewed Mishima as less the literary man and more the patriot and loyal friend. He often said he found the purest expression of Japan's spirit among the defense forces. So he was given free access to military bases as well as special permission to train with his youth corps at military campsites. And when Mishima ended his life, he did so not at his writing studio but at the Eastern Corps Headquarters of the Ground Self-Defense Forces, in the Ichigaya section of Tokyo.

The Society of Shields had nothing literary about it. Its members did not even read Mishima's books. After his death and ritual beheading, as well as the sacrifice of one of his disciples, it was learned that most members of his youth corps preferred to read comic books.

In Japanese history, a curious intimacy exists between poetry and the fighting man. Before engaging the enemy or before ritual suicide many a samurai warrior of the past or army general of more recent history first sat down and wrote a poem or two. Lafcadio Hearn in his volume *In Ghostly Japan,* written in 1889, comments on this literary bent of warriors.

Another example is General Maresuke Nogi, who fought

the Russians at Port Arthur in 1904 (in the terribly bloody battle, two of Nogi's sons met their deaths). He became known as the "god of the army" but has also been called a sensitive poet for his brief literary efforts. At the death of Emperor Meiji, Nogi committed hara-kiri after first helping his wife to end her life with a dagger.

After Mishima's death, Professor Mimitada Miwa, of Tokyo's Sophia University, wrote: "The ritualistic form of suicide has long been considered the most manly form of action in the whole indigenous culture of Japan." Mishima not only exalted ritual suicide in his works but even produced a short film entitled *Patriotism*. The film, based on his short story of the same name, is about a young officer who kills himself in the ritual way, together with his bride. The background for Mishima's story is the historical incident of February 1936 when young officers staged a bloody but abortive *coup d'état*. Mishima had a fondness for heroic military men, and he especially liked Takamori Saigo, who led an army of rebellion against the Meiji government in 1877 and finally committed suicide with his officers.

Mishima's death had a few political consequences. Police quickly declared they were putting the Society of Shields on their list of subversive rightist organizations and would henceforth keep its members under watch, even though the society had officially disbanded.

In 1971, one candidate for the Tokyo governor's race, an ultranationalist agitator named Bin Akao, said Mishima's death gave him inspiration and courage. To help another candidate, a conservative, in the same campaign, Mishima's name and that of Nobel Laureate Yasunari Kawabata were used, though in a losing cause. A campaign document contained this prize statement:

"Beautiful Japan is being destroyed by leftist forces. You will be surprised to find that many of Mr. Kawabata's reasons for taking part in the election campaign are closely related to those which led Yukio Mishima to commit his protest suicide late last year." Kawabata himself committed suicide by gas inhalation on April 16, 1972.

To commemorate Mishima's death, the nationalistic-minded author and critic, Fusao Hayashi, together with a right-wing student group, helped found the Mishima Research Institute. A part of the new institute's prospectus said:

Japanese history has been shunted to the sidelines, the traditions neglected and the warrior spirit lost. In these modern times of unprecedented degeneration, the Japanese nation has at last burst out of the years that had bottled up its real anger.

The prospectus went on to say that the institute will do all it can to stir up patriotic fervor and will

defend against revolution the Emperor, who constitutes the core of Japanese history, culture and tradition . . . [and will] make a national army out of the Self-Defense Forces in keeping with the basic principle of founding an army; and will enhance the glorious spirit of the Japanese nation.

Mishima often spoke out on the spiritual, social, and political conditions of Japan. He once wrote: "The Japanese people began to decline in morality in 1876 with the decree abolishing the wearing of swords for men." He also said: "Unless everyone comes to have the spirit of being ready to take a rifle and stand up, in case of emergency, Japan will come to a sad predicament in the future." He believed postwar society had become perverted because "it has lost uniforms." For him, uniforms were "indispensable for the expression of ideas."

In short, Mishima's ideas are very nearly the quintessence of militarism.

Mishima said democracy had two principal defects. First, it had no roots in Japanese history and, second, it was of "no service at all" in preserving Japan's cultural traditions or in maintaining the purity of Japanese history. He said: "I do not think democracy will guarantee what we must defend. And I also do not think that the defending of democracy will ultimately ensure what we must defend."

And what is it that must be defended? The warrior-poet, who always wore his hair cropped short, military style, spares no effort to tell us. In his 1968 essay, "In Defense of Culture," which runs to some forty pages, he uses ten pages to explain the Emperor as a cultural concept. It is hard reading. The U.S. Ambassador to Japan at that time, U. Alexis Johnson, wishing to decipher the meaning, asked his specialists, and was told that Mishima wished to see an almost complete return to the prewar Imperial system, with its taut web of loyalties. But, Johnson was informed, this would not be likely to happen for some years and surely not during his tenure of office. The envoy is said to have breathed a sigh of relief.

For Mishima, Japanese culture embraces not only art works but also patterns of behavior. It includes:

> Noh drama
> Kabuki
> Memorabilia left behind by kamikaze suicide pilots
> The action of a naval officer who jumped out of a manned torpedo which surfaced in the South Pacific, holding a Japanese sword, and was killed in action
> *Tales of Genji*
> *Manyoshu* (ancient anthology of verse)

> Kendo and judo images of Buddha in the Chuson-ji Temple, near Sendai, founded in A.D. 1105
> Modern sculpture
> Soldiers' deportment (loyalty, valor, etc.)
> *Yakuza* (gangsters') sword-play movies
> Zen
> Flower arranging and tea ceremony
> Modern novels and poetry

Whether or not he intended it, he includes his own literary work by listing modern novels and poetry. Nevertheless, Mishima held a low opinion of Japan's modern *belles-lettres*. He once wrote: "Japanese [modern] literature is a paradise of insomniacs, neurotics, impotents, ugly masses of fat, cancer and stomach disease patients, sentimentalists and semilunatics. Those who can fight are few." It comes close to sounding like a page from Nietzsche.

I once met him for dinner at a Tokyo restaurant and put a number of questions to him. Mishima was true to his reputation as a man who dressed stylishly. He wore a black silk suit with cream-colored tie. His manner was bland, he laughed easily and hastily dismissed things with which he disagreed. He spoke in precise English. Here are the questions and his replies:

Question: Is it true that the formation of Tate no Kai, which is a private organization, is your personal attempt to protect the people living in Japan who in theory have no military forces?

Mishima (smiling): In order to have adequate defense power, including manpower, it becomes indispensable to have the cooperation of a militia. Tate no Kai is the basis of such a militia. To tell the truth, I may be unrealistic, but I wanted the revival of traditional Japanese nationalism and the samurai spirit to come true today.

Question: Is this not *Bushido* [the "way of the warrior"]?

Mishima: That's right.

Question: But don't you have any fear your military or its thought might be misinterpreted or misused?

Mishima: I don't think so.

Question: But I do think there could be danger. In fact, about thirty-five years ago there was a dangerous incident—the February 26 young officers' revolt—wasn't there?

Mishima: Our organization is not fascistic. It is very free. Furthermore, our group has about one hundred young men with a radical idea but with no intention of enlarging its membership.

Question: The strategy you have in mind is guerrilla warfare, isn't it?

Mishima: No, it's not, provided Japan is not invaded indirectly. In other words, our idea is to foster a good leader who can stand up at the head of ten or so volunteer youths, in cooperation with the SDF in the event of some improper elements trying to break away or cause a civil war. Our members [Tate no Kai] are one hundred, but they possess the power equal to that of a thousand in times of emergency.

Question: In my opinion, the reason you formed the Tate no Kai was due to your fear toward existing anti-Japanese or antitraditional thinking among some Japanese. Is this true?

Mishima: That's it. Besides, I hate the timidity of the Japanese.

Was Mishima bragging when he talked about the strength of his youth corps? Evidently not, because during the Mishima Incident he and only four of his young followers were able to take control, for a limited period, of the Eastern District Headquarters of Japan's national army, even though several thousand men were on hand. Mishima and his band performed this feat by making a prisoner of the commanding general.

Mishima's loathing for any kind of weakness, or pacifism, has parallels in certain ancient traditions. Moreover, in a characteristic fusillade, Mishima paired public opinion with women and nuclear weapons with men. He went on to say that nuclear weapons are "controlled by public opinion," and men, he adds wryly, "are always under the control of women."

From this improbable premise, he arrived at the conclusion: "If you wish to win, you must be weak or a victim." And further: "It is so arranged that women will certainly win."

One may consider such thinking a kind of aberration, or pure fantasy; but Mishima was actually in step with a rising opinion among zaibatsu and ruling-party leaders that it is essential for Japan to possess nuclear weapons so that Japan will not be inferior to the superpowers. It is only that Mishima's words are more extreme.

The professional right-wing politicians were pleased when Mishima, the popular writer, lent his support to their causes. Even if his speech and writings seemed intemperate, Japan's ultraconservative leaders could find common ground with Mishima.

In an article he wrote for the business journal *Nikkeiren Times* (the organ of the Japan Federation of Employers' Associations), Mishima is conservative to the bone. The article, titled, "My Assertions for Self-Defense," says that is the "mirror which reflects all." And it is the duty of all the people wholly to reject those elements in the society that do not derive from Japanese culture, history, or traditions—for instance, Communists and Marxist intellectuals.

Anti-Communism made a subtle entrance into Mishima's literary works. In *Harp of Joy,* a drama written in the early 1960's, a clash occurs between leftists and rightists, and there are some tough anti-Communist lines. At a rehearsal, an actor who had to speak these lines was suddenly overcome, saying: "I can't read them." Mishima is alleged to have coaxed him to stick it out, presumably in the name of art.

Another anecdote reveals both Mishima's hatred of the left wing and his fondness for the ancient warrior code. In 1960, all Japan was jolted by the slaying of the popular chairman of the Japan Socialist Party, Inejiro Asanuma, by a teen-aged right-wing fanatic. Taken to a police cell, the young assassin later used his belt to hang himself. Mishima hailed the youth for his political murder and willingness to pay for his deed with his own life. It was, in Mishima's eyes, "complete," "perfect," and "in the Japanese tradition." Most rightist groups nodded their approval of the young man's deed.

If one probes for the source of Mishima's fanaticism, one finds a major part of it in Bushido, the chivalry of the feudal warrior. Several books reveal in absorbing detail the essence and rituals of Japan's samurai past.

Bushido embraces simple militarism. It stresses the warrior ideals of readiness for combat, self-sacrifice, and loyalty. Bushido taught that the samurai's sword was the tangible expression of his honor, which was dearer to him than his life. In this code, it is said that too much attachment to life is craven. Discipline for warriors, pared down to its basic component, means to be ready to die.

When Mishima said that "a Japanese sword once unsheathed must not be replaced until it has cut through something or someone," he was paraphrasing what was said several centuries ago by leading samurai.

The image of the feudal warrior is presented in *Hagakure* (*Hidden Behind the Leaves*), a remarkable volume on samurai ethics which Mishima knew almost by heart. Written by an eighteenth-century monk, it says that Bushido is nothing but how to die. Honor means fighting to the bitter end; surrender is equated with dishonor. It is only at the instant when one determines to die that a man attains true purity; a harsh code, indeed.

This gripping passage goes right to the core:

When one is forced to choose between life and death, it is important to choose death without hesitation. There should be no elaborate reasoning. Simply decide and act. The idea that it is meaningless to die without accomplishing one's aims is a frivolous and despicable one, characteristic of those Kamigata (Kyoto and Osaka) people. It would be impossible to make a reasoned judgment when the choice hangs between life and death. We prefer to live when the choice hangs between life and death. We all prefer to live rather than die. So we would probably argue that what we want most is right. However, if one lives on to face the failure to accomplish one's aims, then one is a coward. To think that one cannot die without accomplishing one's aims is vain indeed. But it is no cause for shame. This and only this is the right way for the *bushi* (warrior-gentleman). If he practices self-examination morning and night, and is prepared to give up his life at any time, then he can be perfect in all the martial arts, and live his whole life perfectly.

One also finds this vivid passage in *Hagakure*:

A man of true valor is the one who leaves his place without a word to meet his death. It is not necessary to kill the opponent. The truly valiant is the one who is slain without uttering a word.

Words like these goaded Mishima to action and formed part of his basic psychology. Often he exhorted his fellow citizens to lay down their lives to recapture the lost glory of the Empire or to kill the Constitution, which he loathed. Such a code, which is like a religion, produced Japan's human bullets, those men who steered torpedoes against enemy ships in World War II, as well as the kamikaze pilots.

Mishima was thoroughly familiar with the literature on Bushido and, in 1967, wrote an essay entitled "The Code of *Hagakure* and I."

Perhaps the most striking side effect of the Mishima Incident was that it revealed a deep vein of antimodernism among many Japanese who have a fondness for heroic action and tradition, even when this leads a prominent native son to perform the barbaric act of ritual suicide. The sympathetic reactions of many persons to Mishima's hara-kiri was, in my opinion, almost as stunning as the act itself. Some of the adjectives that were used to describe the act included "sublime," "aesthetic," "beautiful," and "pure." One intellectual compared Mishima's self-sacrifice to the crucifixion of Christ.

China reacted at length to Mishima's suicide, calling it proof of a resurgent Japanese militarism. China continues to be suspicious of the big-power mentality held by leading Japanese who say Japan can fulfill its destiny only by possessing great military power.

The death of Yukio Mishima caused some Japanese to think how they might escape their heritage. They wondered how they might challenge what one Japanese writer called a "legacy of repression."

Even before the grotesque suicide, there were some Japanese who spoke of going beyond being a Japanese. For example, popular author and antiwar critic Makoto Oda said it was his right as a human being to choose not to be Japanese, if that was his wish. He wrote: "The advance and growth of human existence is far more important to me than that of the organism called Japan." Of course, Oda's voice belongs to a minority.

5

The Superpatriots

The right wing is associated with divine inspiration and with Japan as the divine land. This leads to militarism.
— Yoshio Kodama, theoretician. Remark made in 1969 interview

It will take at least three more years for the right wing to be trusted and loved by the country.
— Yoshio Kodama (1969)

Nobody can dare to predict that such insanity will not again infect the body politic of Japan.
— Richard Storry, British historian, commenting on the attempted military *coup d'états* in the 1930's. From *The Double Patriots,* 1957

Several students who idolized Yukio Mishima and had apparent ultranationalist leanings followed Mishima's example and disemboweled themselves. So did a Buddhist priest of the Taiun-ji Temple, near Kobe.

Even an American student performed this barbarous rite, although it was difficult to know whether the young man was a fan of Mishima's or a votary of the Bushido cult. A year after Mishima's suicide, police stopped a man who tried to commit hara-kiri in front of the Ichigaya military headquarters in Tokyo, where Mishima had taken his own life.

Only a month after the Mishima Incident, a local newspaper commented: "Hara-kiri seems to be in vogue in Japan. . . ."

One fanatic student committed hara-kiri and, after he had cut open his abodmen, tried to behead himself. This savagery took place in a fine-arts museum where an exhibition of ancient swords was on display. Mishima was addicted to swords, as are many ultranationalists.

To kill himself, this student, a twenty-three-year-old philosophy major, broke open a glass display case and chose a rare sword fashioned in the thirteenth century by Masamune, one of Japan's famed swordsmiths. After warning spectators to stay away from him, the student gashed his abdomen and then his neck as thirty-odd viewers watched helplessly.

Such a gruesome act is portrayed by the nineteenth-century painter E-kin in a lurid painting which was used as promotional material for a recent movie about the life of this artist.

Ultrarightists in Japan have sometimes killed themselves to create sympathy for their cause, or to protest a certain action. Earlier in the twentieth century, one ultranationalist committed suicide to show his anger at the American alien-exclusion acts of the 1920's, which were aimed at stemming the flow of Japanese and Chinese immigrants to the United States. In 1959, when Crown Prince Akihito broke with tradition and married a commoner, Miss Michiko Shoda, a man with strong nationalist and traditionalist feelings killed himself in protest.

In 1969, a rightist youth burned himself to death near the Imperial Palace. He was the great-grandson of the late statesman, Shimpei Eto, who led a rebellion against the regime of the Emperor Meiji. In a suicide note, the youth said he wished to "awaken the Japanese people to the significance of the spiritual heritage of the Empire." The youth, who had served briefly in the Self-Defense Forces, also said: "I am taking my own life on National Foundation Commemoration Day [February 11] so that my message will be heard loud and clear."

These are only a few examples. Leftist-inclined persons also take their lives to support their beliefs, although suicide is much less common among the political left than among the right. To show disapproval of the Prime Minister's trip to America in 1967, an elderly man with left-wing sympathies burned himself fatally.

During his life, Mishima appears to have kept a discreet aloofness from the radical right. In death, however, the ultraright eulogized him. If rightists believed a liberal scholar or writer was about to make a speech in which he might criticize Mishima, they would issue threats against the speaker or the sponsors of the gathering, and the speech was sometimes cancelled. By making a prickly nuisance of itself, the right wing in Japan is often able to achieve its objectives.

The right wing received a temporary blow from Japan's World War II defeat, but it bounced back nimbly. Upon Japan's surrender, General MacArthur "dissolved forever" over two hundred of approximately 350 patriotic and nationalistic societies. No fewer than 200,000 militarists and rightists who had helped shape the nation's warlike policies were purged. But by the first postwar general elections in 1946, at least 193 ultranationalist groups were back in business, in addition to others which had survived by repainting their signboards.

The National Police Agency now lists 460 active right-wing organizations with a membership of 140,000. An almanac on the Japanese right wing indicates that its total strength, including those who are sympathetic with these organizations, exceeds 2.5 million, in addition to 300,000 students who belong to patriotic clubs. Police say there are about 15,000 hard-core rightists; that is, those who will not hesitate to use terrorist tactics.

The Korean War and General MacArthur's purge of Japanese Communists provided a helping hand for the resurgent right wing. Even today, rightists are proud of the encouraging words they received from high U.S. officials. For example, ultranationalist Wataru Shimizu likes to show a letter from the late Secretary of State John Foster Dulles dated July 1950 which ends: ". . . I hope that you will continue your efforts against Communism."

The basic mental attitudes of the wartime Japanese *gumbatsu*—or militarist clique—and the civilian right-wing extremists who together led the nation to war were characterized by a constant appeal to force and violence, a deification of power, and a longing for revenge. Such attitudes persist among present-day ultranationalist groups.

As to specific goals, they support the following:

Restoration of the Emperor as head of state
The build-up of a powerful military, including nuclear weapons
A ban on the Communist and other left-wing parties
Revision of the antiwar Constitution
State subsidies for Shinto shrines

In 1946 the Education Ministry tried to root out militaristic ideas from the schools by publishing a Guide to New Education in Japan. This guide said that in order to create a new Japan it was important to rid the nation of militarism and ultranationalism. Specifically, it stated:

It is by reorienting the attitude and sentiment of the Japanese people, and by no other means, that militarism and ultranationalism can fundamentally and eternally be eliminated.

For this purpose, it offered a list of do's and don't's. A few examples:

Whatever it may be about, it is not well to obey orders blindly from above.
There must be no instigation of the people to be vexed at defeat and to brood upon vengeance.
The custom of beginning to fight at the slightest provocation must be stopped.

Many of these ideas were worlds apart from what had been fed to youths during the prewar and wartime period. As far back as 1932, the Education Ministry, noting a leftist trend among students, had blamed it on such habits as credulity, a sense of justice, a lust for knowledge, and curiosity and an imitative nature.

With the reverse trend that emerged during and after the U.S. Occupation, many formerly active ultranationalists reappeared on the public stage. They seem to have had little trouble in attracting eager young partisans. Today the ranks of the right-wing leadership include Buddhist priests, teachers in rural schools, small businessmen, local politicians, and ex-soldiers. All are steeped in patriotism and the traditional values.

Most ultrarightist chieftains have gone through elementary and secondary school but not beyond. Many are firstrate orators who can hold a large audience spellbound, especially if it consists of naïve youths and workingmen. They live on generally meager wages but, being zealots, they thrive on a spartan regimen. Many engage in daily practice of the martial arts. Most, if not all, give a certain portion of each day to reciting Buddhist sutras, or sit in Zen meditation. Their home life appears to be bleak. Their allegiance is to Emperor, flag, and country; everything else is of lesser importance.

Yoshio Kodama is one of the prominent rightists who made a successful comeback from a cell in Tokyo's Sugamo Prison, where he spent three years as a Class-A War Criminal. His credo on patriotism is simple: "Shed your blood for the state, shed tears for your friends, and sweat for your family." At present, Kodama sits at or near the top of Japan's rightist hierarchy.

The mere mention of Kodama's name occasions frowns among many Japanese citizens. Kodama, born in 1911, was a wartime manipulator and an undercover agent. He gained money and power through his Kodama Organ in China, which procured supplies for the Japanese Navy.

When the Sino-Japanese War began, he was virtually without a yen in his pocket. Yet, when the war ended, his assets in Japan were worth—by his own reckoning—150 million yen (over $400,000).

Withal, Kodama is no fanatic; he even says he hates simple terrorism. He once said that he was sorry to hear of the rightist assassination of Socialist Party Chairman Inejiro Asanuma, with whom he sometimes used to drink *sake*. Kodama is a rightist intellectual and theorist. He advises numerous ultranationalist societies, including important youth groups.

Of all contemporary ultrarightists, Kodama is probably the best known by his fellow citizens. Another famous ultranationalist was the late Ikki Kita, whose notoriety and extremism between the two world wars was unsurpassed. Kita has been called a Fascist by Japanese scholars; and Dr. Masao Maruyama, one of Japan's most distinguished political scientists, considers Kita the intellectual father of Japanese Fascism. Kita was implicated in a military coup plot in 1936 and died by a firing squad.

Kodama and Kita reflect many of the strange and diverse elements and vicissitudes of the right-wing nationalist movement in Japan.

Kita (1883–1937) was a tragic figure. He was elitist; fanatic, mystical, and solitary. Daily, he would recite Buddhist sutras out loud. He was also an aggressive militarist and expansionist. Japan, he said, had the right to seize other territory to ease population pressure and, also, to drive the Western imperialists from Asia. In his chief literary effort, *Nihon Kaizo Hoan Taiko* (*General Outline for the Reconstruction of Japan*), Kita urged the seizure of additional territory, the establishment of martial law in Japan, and the suspension of the Constitution so that the Emperor could rule without hindrance, and thus effect badly needed domestic reforms.

Kita and Kodama have traits in common. Both were China experts, having lived in China and been intimate with Chinese politics and history. In their youth, both were angry young men who knew the inside of police jails. Both were complex personalities, Kita more so than Kodama.

Both embraced apparent contradictions. In their statements, each was bitterly against capitalism. Yet, in the 1930's, Kita rationalized his acceptance of big sums of money from the Mitsui zaibatsu; Kodama, whose hatred of corrupt party politics and big business stemmed from his youthful hard knocks as a factory laborer, made a fortune in the Sino-Japanese War and at its end was actually an adviser to the ruling conservative party. As a result, a few old friends accused him of selling out.

Ikki Kita wished to bring the Emperor and the people closer together. So does Kodama. When he was only eighteen years old, Kodama volunteered to approach the Emperor to hand him a petition that sought help for 2 million jobless persons—it was 1929—and also assailed a new, left-oriented farmer-labor party. He was arrested on the spot.

Kita actually wished to see some reforms. In his book on Japan's reconstruction, he called on the Emperor to grant part of his landholdings to the nation, and he recommended that the Emperor's yearly expenses be reduced. Such views were, of course, quite radical, and from time to time the police were knocking on his door. Kita's controversial ideas appealed to many youths, including military officers, who were angered by contradictions in society. And with the fanaticism of patriots, they were often willing to follow reformist leaders like Kita.

After the war, Kodama showed flexibility in his thinking about the Emperor. In an interview, Kodama said that the Emperor "does not necessarily have to be 'head' of state. It is sufficient—nay, it is perhaps better—that he is a 'symbol' of the state as the current Constitution says." Such a view is certainly not held by the rank and file of the ultra-right. In this concept, Kodama's individuality and candor are revealed.

In addition to mysticism, Kita portrayed a national arrogance and conceit. Only Japan, he said, was capable of showing China and India the correct path, and, for such leadership, Japan needed the gospel of the sword. World War I, for Kita, was "punishment from heaven" brought upon the Europeans.

Kita saw war and suffering as part of an immense religious spectacle. Kodama was different. After the war, he criticized the brutality and inhumanity of Japanese militarism, especially in China. But according to statements in his book, *I Was Defeated,* Kodama was offended by such horrors even during the war. Kodama, too, shows a mystical streak. In his book he says that "peace and war are dominated by a power far greater than man himself."

In sum, Ikki Kita remains an incendiary radical in modern Japanese history whose influence lingers among some postwar rightists. Interestingly, elder statesman Nobusuke Kishi, a postwar Prime Minister who presently wields considerable power within the Liberal Democratic Party, admits that Kita had a serious influence on him during his university days. Kishi says he once reproduced

Kita's revolutionary book on reconstructing Japan, a work of several hundred pages, ideograph by ideograph.

A curious note: Kodama once said militaristic nationalism died with Japan's unconditional surrender in August 1945. Yet more recently he said that the right wing is growing rapidly and that its emphasis on Japan as a divine land leads straight to militarism.

Another right-wing leader is Bin Akao, president of the *Dai Nippon Aikokuto* (Greater Japan Patriotic Party). Akao shows none of the stature or moderation of Kodama. White-haired and seventy-three years old in 1972, Akao is a tireless agitator and street campaigner.

Once, in a panel discussion in 1961, Akao called on youth to trust him implicitly. "Commit murder when I tell you to," he said. Police have chastised him several times for publicly suggesting that leading liberals, such as Tokyo Governor Dr. Ryokichi Minobe, be assassinated.

Already, two youths who were affiliated with Akao's patriotic group have committed murder, although Akao denies any responsibility. One was the killer of Socialist Party Chairman Asanuma. Another youth, Kazutaka Komori, stabbed the wife of a prominent Tokyo publisher because an article in her husband's magazine allegedly slighted the Imperial family. The youth killed a housemaid in the assault.

Bin Akao once gave this incongruous list of those whom he said he worships: South Korean President Park Chung Hee, Jesus Christ, Hitler, Buddha, and Emperor Meiji. (The young slayer of the Socialist leader told police he was an avid reader of Hitler's *Mein Kampf*, and before he hanged himself in his cell in 1960, he said he worshiped the Nazi Fuehrer.)

Another notable ultranationalist, Yoshiaki Sagoya, ten years younger than Akao, is well known for his shooting of Prime Minister Osachi Hamaguchi at Tokyo Station in 1930. Hamaguchi later died from his gunshot wound, and Sagoya served a short jail term. Nowadays he is not the least bit penitent. "I shot Prime Minister Hamaguchi myself, but I don't regret it at all," he has said.

Sagoya leads a Spartan life. He is a karate expert, takes no breakfast, endures cold showers, rises at five and is in bed by ten. He recites Buddhist prayers daily—like Ikki Kita—and sits in Zen meditation for a half hour.

He is adviser to *Gokoku Dan* (Defense of the Fatherland Corps), and is chairman of the All-Japan Federation of Rightist and Patriotic Organizations, which claims affiliation with more than four hundred right-wing groups, with over 120,000 members.

All these ultrarightist chieftains are involved with bringing forth young believers, nourished on fanaticism and a sense of national crisis. The following is not an unusual occurrence. Recently there was a study meeting held at Togakushi Plateau, in Nagano Prefecture, northwest of Tokyo, in which seventy persons from nineteen ultranationalist societies participated. Part of the study meeting included military training sessions, sometimes in heavy rain, which did not deter the members, most of whom were young company clerks whose average age was about twenty-five. The training was intense, with the newcomers being taught to dispose of five persons each in case of a clash with the enemy.

Who pays the bills? Who provides the money for the study meetings, the lodges where the youths stay, their meals, transportation, and so on?

It is often said that the extreme right in Japan exists and

even thrives because of the various forms of aid from the Liberal-Democratic Party and big business. There are links between them, though perhaps not as extensive as sometimes charged.

Many zaibatsu industrialists share the basic beliefs of the superpatriots. Moreover, the ruling Liberal-Democratic Party, which is indubitably the party of big business, has not stopped at summoning notorious right-wing leaders for help in bailing the party out of political crises.

Some of the ultrarightist rank and file find jobs in large companies whose chief executives are friendly with right-wing bosses or sympathetic to their cause. A few militant right-wing groups try extortion and blackmail to obtain money from rich businessmen. Racketeers with close ties to right-wing societies supply guards to protect factories or serve at stockholders' meetings to keep out left-wing radicals who wish to disrupt the gatherings. Thus, one discovers a variety of ties between the extreme right wing and the zaibatsu.

A surprising amount of effort has been expended by the conservative party to get the cooperation of ultranationalist and gangster manpower. The two groups overlap. Almost all gangster elements in Japan belong to ultrarightist organizations or are inclined toward the extreme right wing. However, the reverse is not true: many professional ultranationalists have nothing in common with the coarse life style of the underworld.

In mid-1960 the Kishi Administration badly needed extra manpower. Prime Minister Nobusuke Kishi was fighting for his political life. Although his position was weak, he nevertheless wished to give a warm welcome to U.S. President Dwight D. Eisenhower and to use the visit to add a glorious finale to his unpopular administration. But there were daily anti-Kishi and anti-security-treaty protest demonstrations that were nearing the level of mass hysteria. The 1960 "demos," as demonstrations are called in Japan, had the possibility of endangering Eisenhower's life if he visited Japan. Many Japanese were angry at the Kishi Administration for forcing ratification of the Japanese-American Security Treaty through the Diet. They felt that the treaty was more a liability than a safety measure for Japan.

Each day the situation became more grave; the demos increased, and the tens of thousands of demonstrators and police outside the Diet Building made it look as if the Diet were under siege. One university coed had been crushed to death in front of the Diet; several hundred persons already had been injured. The situation appeared to be getting out of hand.

The police could mobilize approximately fifteen thousand men to protect "Ike." But thousands more were needed to guard the road from the airport to the heart of Tokyo. Eisenhower and Emperor Hirohito were scheduled to ride together from the airport.

One man called in to help was Yoshio Kodama. He has said he controls about 60 per cent of the Japanese right wing, although some observers say it is closer to 90 per cent if, for example, he wished to recruit rightist activists under the banner of anti-Communism. Reports say that about $2.3 million was pledged by businessmen, racketeers, and right-wing groups to Operation Protect Ike. This money was to be used to provide helicopters, trucks, cars, and first-aid stations to the hired right-wing guards.

The Prime Minister is said to have considered calling out the Self-Defense Forces, but was wisely counseled against this move by one of his aides. The pent-up feelings of the protesters would likely have burst forth if the military had been called out, probably resulting in an extremely dangerous situation. In any case, the Eisenhower visit was finally canceled because it was considered to be too risky.

But the aborted plan contained an omen for the future. A well-organized and disciplined body of ultranationalists plus gangster elements could, with the avowed backing of the ruling party, help serve as a powerful counterweight against a dissident population.

In 1965, when a keen political debate raged in Japan over whether or not to sign a normalization treaty with South Korea, the National Police Agency expressed shock at the blatant efforts of the Liberal-Democratic Party to solicit help from ultrarightists and underworld elements. Police said the ruling party met on at least two occasions with such elements at a well-known inn at Akasaka, in downtown Tokyo. Prominent lawmakers addressed the gatherings, which included sixty-odd rightists and gang bosses. Among the organizations present were *Gijin-to* (The Martyrs' Party); *Dai Nippon Aikokuto* (Greater Japan Patriotic Party); and *Gokoku Dan* (Defense of the Fatherland Corps).

The government and the conservative party were eager to have the normalization treaty ratified in the Diet after many years of wrangling between Japan and South Korea in the postwar era. However, there were huge demonstrations in protest in the cities as the Diet began deliberations on the treaty. The demonstrators included the militant *Zengakuren* (All-Japan Federation of Student Organizations), the Socialists, Communists, labor-union members, as well as many liberals and intellectuals who opposed the treaty because it proclaimed the Seoul regime as the legal government for the whole of Korea. This, claimed the treaty's opponents, would perpetuate the division of North and South Korea.

To insure victory and to help silence the left-wing opposition, the party bosses sought the aid of the extreme right wing and the underworld in distributing leaflets. They were also used as a muscular counterforce to the left wing. The strategy of the ruling party was successful, but police were aghast. They said many of the groups that the ruling party contacted were high on the police antisocial blacklist.

Today's nationally organized police are anti-Communist, and it might seem they would side more with the right wing than with the liberals and leftists. One may get the impression of awesome police power in Japan because of the many platoons of riot police seen frequently on the main streets with their helmets, shields, and truncheons. Sometimes five thousand or even ten thousand riot police, or *kidotai*, are called to preserve order. But the police do not unduly harass the left as they did in prewar days.

Strict and meticulous compliance with the law has been a tradition in Japan despite many infractions, intentional or not, by the authorities. Because of the public's lingering distrust of police, which stems from wartime police repression, the police since the U.S. Occupation have striven to regain the public's confidence by attempting to be impartial in upholding the law. Each year, the police agency issues reports on the dangers to the nation from both the extreme right and the extreme left.

In the 1965 incident, the police actually issued a complaint, saying: "It is very regrettable to know that there were such ruling party moves which encourage organized antisocial activities at the same time that police are struggling to exterminate them."

Bonds similar to those linking the Japanese underworld and the right wing are scarcely visible in most other advanced countries. An example in Japan is *Matsubakai,* or Pine Needle Society. It is a gangster-rightist organization that was formed in 1953 with three thousand members, comprising three huge groups of gamblers whose activities were spread over a third of Japan. In the 1960 antigovernment demonstrations, many Pine Needle members clashed physically with the protesters.

Pine Needle bosses have rubbed shoulders with distinguished visitors from abroad. For example, when South Korean President Park Chung Hee or his Prime Minister, Kim Chong Pil, visit Tokyo, one of their callers may be a man from Pine Needle or a similar organization.

During a visit to Japan in the mid-1960's, President Park was greeted by some ten thousand cheering spectators at Tokyo's International Airport. These "spectators" were actually members of gangs mobilized for the occasion. One gang boss, Uichiro Fujita, formerly associated with Pine Needle, met Park at his Tokyo hotel and presented him with a hundred transistor radios when the President indicated that some Korean villages were without radios.

There are many right-wing ties between Japan and South Korea. For example, each year hundreds of Japanese young men imbued with intense patriotism join in rifle practice on Korea's Cheju Island, situated between the two nations. Such gatherings are called hunting rallies for the purpose of promoting Japanese-Korean friendship. In mid-1971, some of Japan's best-known ultrarightist leaders, including Bin Akao and Ryoichi Sasagawa, visited South

Korea (and also Taiwan) as part of a big rightist delegation. Sasagawa, who heads the 130,000-member Japan War Wounded Veterans Association, is reported to be on friendly terms with such influential ruling party figures as Nobusuke Kishi and Takeo Fukuda.

In Japan, each underworld gang has its own code, and anti-Communism is a major component. Here are the opening words to the code of the Pine Needle Society: "We the Japanese people are determined to resist the invasion by tyrannical Communism."

The code calls for teaching the Samurai spirit to the youth, and for opposing *Nikkyoso*—the Japan Teachers' Union—because it is "imbued with dangerous thoughts and subversive ideas." This left-oriented union is a periodic target of attack, and its annual convention is invariably an occasion for clashes with rightist groups. At a convention in 1971, a group of rightists hid themselves in the rafters of the meeting hall and poured chemical nontoxic foam onto the stage, terrifying the 2,700 assembled teachers.

A final word on the Pine Needle Society. It went through an ostensible dissolution ceremony in 1965, complete with religious rites, held at the Hoshoji Temple in Tokyo. But police say that offshoots of the parent body still exist. Also, an affiliate organization was formed and duly registered as a political party prior to the dissolution. The new organization's members encompassed nearly all of the Pine Needle Society. Many underworld groups have formed political organizations that supposedly give the members a new respectability.

A remarkable marriage of the ultraright and the underworld took place in December 1963 at an Atami hotsprings resort near Tokyo. At this wedding, powerful gangland chiefs joined together into one politically ultra-rightist organization called *Kantokai*. The meeting opened with the singing of *Kimigayo,* the national anthem, and ended with shouts of banzai ("Live ten thousand years!") for the Emperor and Empress. Conspicuously present was Yoshio Kodama.

Kodama, who was once employed as a bodyguard for an eminent Chinese politician, addressed this audience of gangland toughs and appealed straightaway to their patriotism. He told them:

Why waste our life and energy for such silly ends as making a fuss whether or not someone jostled you, or whether or not you lost face? Instead, why not think of things which may contribute to the good of the world and the country? When we have scuffles, before we shed our blood let us solve them by discussion. Let us only use our physical strength when we are in danger of a leftist revolution in Japan.

This new organization, too, drew up a code which included these statements: "Kantokai challenges Communism and expects to eradicate it, seeking at the same time to enhance a patriotic spirit among our people." Also: "Kantokai shall endeavor to promote international cooperation with Asian nations that are on the side of the Free World, and hopes for the realization of a confederation of Asia." Certainly this is an echo, however faint, of the erstwhile Greater East-Asia Co-prosperity Sphere, which Japan tried to establish through armed might.

One gang boss who was present at Atami said later: "We gamblers cannot walk in broad daylight, but if we unite and become a wall to stop Communism, we can be of service to the nation. If anything happens, we would like to stake our lives for the good of the country." Kodama's demagogic approach had apparently paid off.

With such ideological fervor, one would naturally expect frequent outbursts of violence against the Communists and the left wing in general. Indeed, attempts are made now and then to murder top Communist leaders as well as other left-wing politicians. Many such leaders have private as well as police bodyguards.

Rightists often harass visiting officials from China and the Soviet Union, especially the latter. When Soviet Deputy Premier Nicolai Baibakov came to Japan in 1968, he was hit over the head with a wooden sword by a young nationalist who said he wanted to "teach the Russians a lesson." One of the youth's uncles had committed suicide with a dozen or so other patriots in August 1945 to protest Japan's surrender.

Anastas Mikoyan, a former Deputy Premier of the Soviet Union, made several visits to Japan and was also troubled by right-wing radicals. When he arrived in Tokyo in 1964, police foiled a rightist plot to dynamite Mikoyan's car as it headed for Tokyo from the airport. During his previous visit to Japan, police took into a custody a rightist youth who had said: "I'll kill Mikoyan and therefore contribute to Japan's future." In a note, the youth demanded that Moscow apologize for violating the Russo-Japanese nonaggression pact in August 1945, when the Soviets entered the war against Japan. Such is the hatred of Russia which pervades the Japanese right wing.

The ultraright also does its best to hurt Tokyo-Peking relations. But since few Chinese leaders visit Japan, the rightists concentrate on disrupting Chinese trade and other exhibits held in Japan. In 1958 they tore down a Chinese flag atop a major Chinese industrial fair in Nagasaki, causing China to cancel existing trade agreements with Japan. Commerce between the two nations actually fell

from above $100 million in 1958 to less than $25 million
the next year. Recently this trade has climbed above $900
million and is likely to eclipse the billion-dollar mark.   ·

What especially irked the Chinese in the Nagasaki flag
incident was that the right-wing Kishi Administration
seemed indifferent to press reports that ultrarightists
would attack the exhibition.

The rightists did everything they possibly could to
torment the Chinese team at the 1971 international ping-
pong tournament at Nagoya, which has become famous
because it led to a thaw in Chinese-American relations.

Despite police vigilance, rightists in Nagoya tore up
portraits of Mao Tse-tung in attempts to antagonize the
Chinese; attacked "pro-Chinese" members of the tournament organizing committee with wooden staves; ignited
smoke bombs at the hotel where the Chinese team was
staying; distributed five thousand anti-Chinese handbills;
set off firecrackers near the hotel; burned Chinese flags;
and telephoned threats to tournament officials.

One ultrarightist boldly demanded more than 1 million
yen from the Japan Table Tennis Association in order
to dissuade his Society of Showa Youths from making
violent attacks on the tournament itself. Police said the
culprit was the same man who had struck Soviet official
Baibakov over the head when he arrived in Japan.

Moreover, this same ultrarightist had already success-
fully extorted more than 400,000 yen (over $1,000) from
one of the organizers of the tournament.

It is not always easy to identify rightist involvement in
incidents that otherwise bear the right-wing imprimatur.
For example, at least two American ambassadors have
been assaulted while at their posts in Japan. One, Dr.
Reischauer, received a nasty stab wound in the right

thigh in 1964. Ambassador Armin H. Meyer was thrown to the ground in 1969 by a youth who wanted all Americans off Japanese soil. Police said in both incidents they could find no known links with the right wing.

Nevertheless, the youth who stabbed Reischauer was an admirer of Hitler and Tojo; also, he blamed U.S. Occupation reforms for destroying Japanese morality. Whether or not the two assailants were bona-fide rightists, their thinking showed parallels with orthodox right-wing ideology.

An important question is whether Japan's new military forces would ever join hands with the politically militant right wing. The exact depth and scope of their present relationship is hard to gauge. Yet there are common interests, since each favors rapid increased armament, and anti-Communism is a common denominator. Already, there are disquieting signs of cooperation.

Hundreds of ultrarightist youths sign on for short training periods at Self-Defense Force bases. Yukio Mishima's rightist youth corps trained actively with the SDF and had privileged access to an army headquarters. Some of the young rightists who committed violence had previously served in the SDF or had family links to the military.

The father of the youth who slew the Socialist Party chairman in 1960 was an SDF officer. The father resigned his post because of the incident. Later he gave a death mask of his son, who had killed himself in a police cell, to a right-wing leader, Wataru Shimizu, who put the mask on his office wall.

More significant is the following fact: an ultranationalist group called the All-Japan Airborne War Comrades Society, consisting of about three thousand members, has actually established its secretariat inside a Japanese Self-

Defense Forces unit at Izumi City, near Osaka. Many of its members are militaristic, anti-Communist activists who wish to return Japan to the prewar authoritarian mold. In 1971, the organization was listed as "undesirable from a security standpoint" by the Osaka Prefectural Police.

6

Japan's Communists

The Communist Party is an enemy of the Self-Defense Forces.

> —Lt. Gen. Ichiro Sugita, Chief of Staff of Ground Self-Defense Forces, in a speech, 1965

In the latter half of the 1970's, the Communist Party will become the strongest challenger of our party.

> —Statement in 1970 by Shojiro Kawashima, late vice president of the ruling Liberal-Democratic Party

Whenever the political skies look especially clear, the Japan Communist Party (JCP) raises the idea of a democratic coalition regime coming to power in the years ahead. Given the archconservatism of the Japanese majority, which includes the better-dead-than-red psychology of the extreme right wing, and the known anti-Communism of the Self-Defense Forces, such a goal would appear very difficult—if not downright hopeless.

Nevertheless, when I asked veteran Communist Kenji Miyamoto, the husky Chairman of the Party, if he felt the red flag would fly over Japan during his lifetime, he said yes; but his reply was carefully worded.

Miyamoto was born in 1908. He seems in robust health. Indeed, he has the build of an ex-miner or a former athlete. In fact, in his high-school days he was a judo champion. At Tokyo Imperial University he was a student of economics, and he joined the Communist Party in 1931.

Miyamoto said: "I think it is possible to create a democratic coalition government in Japan before I die." Quoting statistics on longevity, he said the average Japanese male has a life expectancy of slightly over seventy years and he was optimistic his party could lead a coalition government within ten years at the latest, or before 1981. Actually, he has said such a regime might be formed within the 1970's.

"I hope" he said, "that Japan will not only have a democratic coalition government but will also march forward on the road to socialism while I live."

But Miyamoto, having lived in a police cell between the years 1933 and 1945, knows a good deal about the difficulties of being a Communist in Japan. So he added the cautious remark: "How it will be in reality depends on many various and complicated factors."

Undoubtedly, one of these factors is how the existing authorities would react to such a coalition, especially the police, the armed forces, and the radical right wing of the ruling party, which includes militant allies among Japan's ultranationalists.

Apart from ideological hatred for Communism, the Self-Defense Forces also have a practical reason for opposing a coalition regime of Communists and Socialists, who would be the basic components of a left-wing regime. Both have declared they would abolish the Self-Defense Forces once a new government was formed and establish instead a kind of national relief corps.

Another complicating factor is the relationship of the Communist Party to the other major opposition parties, such as the Socialists and *Komeito* (Clean Government Party), particularly the latter, since Communists and Socialists have often cosponsored political candidates. Komeito remains essentially anti-Communist and therefore is at odds with Miyamoto's party. Komeito is a virile party with a strong ethical tinge, being linked to the Soka Gakkai.

One of the bright, younger members of the Communist Party's Central Committee, Tetsuzo Fuwa (born in 1930), says a precondition for a coalition regime is the elimination of the anti-Communist postures of the Komeito and the Democratic Socialist parties. Fuwa is a popular campaigner who has helped give the Communist Party a new image.

Miyamoto also said that he hoped Komeito would not be especially stubborn in its anti-Communism. Yet, for their part, the Communists have sometimes savagely attacked Soka Gakkai-Komeito. This antipathy was especially obvious in an incident a few years ago when the Communists accused Soka Gakkai-Komeito of violating freedom of speech by trying to suppress a book that was sharply critical of Soka Gakkai and was to be published during a crucial election campaign.

Later the Communists waved the olive branch. For instance, in an article in *Red Flag,* the Communist Party newspaper, Miyamoto offered backhanded praise to Soka Gakkai, saying there were men of good sense in the organization, and he hoped such persons would not become "part of the anti-Communist, nonprogressive current, but part of the current of a democratic, unifying force, including the JCP." He added: "We can hope for this in view of the fact that the number of workers among the Soka Gakkai is not small."

But a precedent was set earlier when Komeito joined forces with the ruling party. Together they beat the leftist parties at Tokyo's gubernatorial polls in 1963. At the time, Komeito's voting strength was about half a million. Therefore, in my opinion, the chances of Komeito's joining a left coalition and the chances for such a movement effectively to challenge the conservative party in the 1970's are quite slim.

In an interview, I asked Miyamoto if he felt Komeito, which is competing with the Socialists as the main opposition party in the National Diet and in local assemblies, was a potential ally or enemy. Again, he replied with care. "We think such a religious party has two possibilities: going in a progressive direction under the influence of the broad masses of working people who support it, or going in an antiworker reactionary direction." But his skepticism was evident when he said he wished to persuade Komeito to carry on the progressive policies they are presenting only on their lips, or in slogans.

If Komeito joined forces with the Communists and Socialists, such a combination might be fatal for the ruling conservatives, who are already a bit anxious over the inroads made by the Communists in national and local elections. Actually, President Daisaku Ikeda of Soka Gakkai has said that the Communists can never be their true ally.

Yet, in the early 1970's, Komeito has shown itself to be a liberal political force, sometimes joining both the Socialists and the Communists in favoring progressive legislation and quick restoration of diplomatic relations with Peking, which is an aspiration of most Japanese.

Japan's Communists are an expanding force. They claim a membership of 300,000. In national elections they are polling up to 5 million votes, roughly 12 per cent of the total. Recently, the Communist Party of Japan has been doing something that is rare among the usually stodgy Communist Parties in the world: it is attempting to modernize and to erase the old image of the party as gloomy and conspiratorial, bent only on violent revolution for Japan.

Even some of the traditional Communist jargon has been thrown out. The word "cell" has been replaced by "branch." The phrase "dictatorship of the proletariat" has been overhauled; party leaders said it gave a misleading image to the public. So instead of translating "dictatorship" directly into Japanese, as was done before, the party decided to use the original Latin word *dictatura* without translation.

In December 1971, the party made some changes to please its membership. It said it would raise salaries for full-time activists and pay them punctually. In the past, delayed payment of salaries had been a source of discontent. In addition, the party said contributions to finance party activities would no longer be compulsory, and activists would be given periodic holidays.

The party has also taken some steps to embrace democracy. It said it wished to seek power through the parliamentary system, and, even after assuming power, it would tolerate opposition parties. Radical leftists sneer at such attitudes.

In addition, the party revised its own constitution in order to ease some of its regulations. The new charter says that under the principle of democratic centralism, those who cannot agree with decisions made by the party have the right to appeal to the Central Committee, with one important condition: dissenters must accept the final decision.

The party opened its 1970 congress for the first time to all segments of the press, and a report on the changes was released in draft form several weeks before the congress convened, in order to solicit members' opinions. The *Red Flag*, which said it received two hundred questions about the draft report, printed answers to many of the questions.

Even *Red Flag* got a face lifting. The paper, with a claimed daily circulation of 400,000, and 1.5 million on Sunday, introduced cartoons and also detective stories by popular writers. The staid character of the theoretical journal was gone. An editor commented that the paper was "designed for everybody, from a five-year-old child to an eighty-five-year-old grandmother."

There was even a rumor about a change in the party's name, perhaps to something like Japan Workers' Party or People's Democratic Party, in order to appeal to a greater number of voters in preparation for a coalition regime.

This new model Communist Party—some have dubbed it "Miyamoto's soft policy line"—is actually quite a break with its past when the party refused to permit dissenters in its ranks and hastily expelled them.

Even the number of women members has increased sharply. Of the 300,000 members, almost one-third are female, almost double the number of a decade ago. Moreover, many of them belong to the postwar generation and, therefore, have no experience with the dark days of the 1920's and 1930's, when members were jailed, or went underground, or sought exile in China and the Soviet Union.

Since the late 1950's, card-carrying members have risen sevenfold, and readers of *Red Flag* have increased forty times. Electoral gains have also been impressive.

In the 1971 gubernatorial polls, those candidates backed jointly by Socialists and Communists triumphed in Tokyo, Osaka, and Kyoto, giving the JCP a ruling share in three giant metropolitan areas. Also, the cities of Yokohama, Kamakura, Kawasaki, and Yokosuka, are governed by men who had joint Socialist-Communist support. In the race for the 23 ward assemblies of Tokyo, also in 1971, the Communists ran 128 candidates—and all were elected. Nationwide, the Communists tripled their seats in prefectural assemblies.

Although the JCP is gaining steadily in National Diet representation, the party's seats in both houses equal less than 5 per cent of the total. And even if the party doubles the number of seats it has in the lower house, as has been predicted, the percentage of the total would still be less than 6 per cent.

Perhaps the biggest question of all, as phrased by cynics, is: How much success can the Communist Party absorb before the "roof caves in"? Many observers are dubious over the party's future, fearing that major gains by the party may cause open clashes with the radical right. The ultraright appears to be biding its time, waiting for a ripe opportunity to go into action.

Often, the party complains about strict police supervision over its activities. In December 1971, the Justice Ministry, in reply to Communist charges, said it had no intention of removing the Communist Party from its list of organizations subject to investigation under the Subversive Activities Prevention Law.

The Communists have often protested in vain. For instance, Chairman Miyamoto complains that his telephone has been tapped by police, and the party disclosed that secret microphones and transmitters have been found in rooms where the party has met, and at the party congress in July 1970.

Also at that congress, the JCP announced that a number of spies had infiltrated the party. Said the Central Committee: "Police actions are becoming more and more cunning."

In the worst possible situation, the top party officials would likely try to flee the country, and it is said that a people's fleet waits in readiness for such an emergency. It is only about four hundred miles between Japan's southernmost main island of Kyushu and China; and, in the north, the distance to Soviet territory is but a few miles. JCP leaders frequently change their residences to escape assassination by fanatical rightists.

Besides the authorities, other elements hinder Communist advances. The zaibatsu is waging its own war against Communism. To educate workers against the left wing, giant firms such as Mitsubishi Heavy Industries and

Sony Corporation issue company bulletins with a circulation of perhaps 200 million (some firms publish more than
one bulletin) whose contents teach that Marxism is obsolete
while capitalism is up-to-date. The firms tell their junior
e ecutives the Communists are enemies of both manage-
ment and labor. One company has shown a newsreel of the
Soviet invasion of Czechoslovakia to all its supervisory
employees as part of an education campaign against Communism.

The Communists are not helped by the fact that Japanese labor is split into left- and right-wing groups. Sohyo
(General Council of Trade Unions) leans to the Socialist
Party and has about 5 million members. It holds that it
will work with the JCP only when they follow the path of
peaceful revolution. Domei (Confederation of Japanese
Labor) is associated with the Democratic-Socialist Party
and has a membership of about 2 million. The Socialist
Party, by the way, is also split into right- and left-wing
factions, with the right wing sometimes dominating the
party.

An economic depression would no doubt assist the goals
of Japan's Communist Party, but no major disruption is
forseen in the 1970's.

The Communist Party of Japan was formed in 1922 and
almost collapsed the following year because of the arrest
and torture of several of its leaders, including the murder
of a few. Among those killed was Sakae Osugi, who had
been a socialist, syndicalist, anarchist, and then a Communist. To Osugi, who was choked to death, every dis-
turbance meant progress if it made the people think.

The two decades before World War II were times of
danger for Communists in Japan. In 1928, in preparation
for the invasion of Manchuria, Prime Minister Giichi

Tanaka went so far as to decree a maximum penalty of death for those convicted of having dangerous thoughts. Many thousands were never tried but languished in police jails.

In 1928 and 1929, police hunted for Communists and sympathizers and rounded up 65,000 persons throughout Japan, including over 2,000 university students. Probably, there were no more than 400 to 500 hard-core Communists in all of Japan in those years.

A revival was attempted in 1931, and approximately seven thousand members were enrolled in the party. During this period, leader Sanzo Nosaka fled to Russia and China, where, in Mao Tse-tung's Yenan caves, he helped start an antiwar league to encourage Japanese soldiers to defect. At this time, Miyamoto was in police detention, not to be released until the end of World War II.

Again, between 1933 and 1936, police arrested 59,013 persons charged with having dangerous thoughts. With the mass arrests, the Communist Party virtually ceased operations.

In the fall of 1945, after Japan's defeat, party leaders and members left their hideouts or jail cells and held a reunion in Tokyo. At first, the party adopted "peaceful revolution" as its slogan and plunged into politics.

For a while, Communist leaders were kindly disposed toward the U.S. Occupation and Americans, even attending dinners now and then with U.S. and other foreign journalists. And the party did well at the polls. In 1949 it elected thirty-five representatives in the National Diet and polled 3 million votes, almost 10 per cent of the total. It was the high-water mark for the party.

Suddenly the party reversed itself in 1950 and showed a violently revolutionary face. The Comintern had attacked the party's pro-imperialist policies, especially criticizing the JCP's conciliatory posture toward the U.S. Occupation. Sanzo Nosaka had previously said a people's government could be set up even under the U.S. Occupation.

Then, in a move that surprised many Japanese, Nosaka publicly recanted and apologized for his alleged errors. And the party switched to militancy, with an extremist wing becoming known for its use of Molotov cocktails.

Meanwhile, the Occupation Forces purged the party's leaders and banned *Red Flag*. American Professor D. M. Brown says there were reports that some ultranationalist societies helped U.S. investigators gather information about Communists in Japan as early as 1948, if not before.

Anti-American riots and violent episodes did much to alienate the party from the masses, and its voting strength dropped to 2 per cent.

Friction has marked the JCP's relations with the Peking regime since the middle 1960's.

In 1966, Kenji Miyamoto visited China and listened to Mao Tse-tung stress the "inevitability of revolution through violence." Miyamoto demurred. Later he began attacking the "great power chauvinists of the Chinese Communist Party" who were "meddling" in Japan's internal affairs. Peking, said Miyamoto, was assuming an attitude of "supreme judge of world revolution."

Miyamoto believes the world situation has changed and that coalition governments of the Communist and other socialist parties can be established through elections, as in Ceylon and Chile. He has said bluntly: "The theory that violent revolution is the sole way to attain the objects of socialism has proved to be a nonscientific and erroneous ideology."

The party's relations with Moscow also have been shaky

in the past, but they seem cordial and even amiable at present. It is noteworthy that Japan's first internationally known Communist, Sen Katayama, lies buried in the Kremlin wall; another Communist, Kyuichi Tokuda, is buried in Peking.

The basic desire of the Japan Communist Party to look after its own house without being told what to do by outsiders is shown by the party's actions at the Soviet Communist Party Congress in 1971. At that time, members of both parties signed a joint communiqué pledging independence and equality for each, and noninterference in the other's domestic affairs. Indeed, the JCP made the strongest plea against monolithic leadership in the Communist world.

Chairman Miyamoto has actually accused China of violating the third principle of the Five Principles of Peaceful Coexistence, first advanced at the Bandung Conference in 1955. The Five Principles are:

1. Mutual respect for each other's territorial integrity and sovereignty.
2. Mutual nonaggression.
3. Mutual noninterference in each other's internal affairs.
4. Equality and mutual benefit.
5. Peaceful coexistence.

Miyamoto says that because of the wretched experiences of the Japanese during World War II, there exists a mood, movement, and opinion that the peace Constitution must be preserved to prevent conscription and overseas dispatch of the nation's armed forces.

According to Miyamoto, militarism is definitely rising and has arrived at a dangerous stage, but it has not yet been completely revived. It is on this issue that Peking has bitterly attacked the JCP, saying it does not sufficiently emphasize the revival of militarism in Japan.

The giant Sohyo labor organization once said Yukio Mishima's hara-kiri suicide might be used as a turning point to justify intervention into politics by the Self-Defense Forces. I asked Miyamoto about this.

According to him, Mishima wished to stimulate rightists and militarists so that in the future they would carry out his desired *coup d'état.* Miyamoto added: "It is true that there is a danger that the rightists in Japan might resort to a *coup d'état* and to terrorism, and there is also a possibility that the revival of Japanese militarism will make further rapid progress."

A recent incident shows how steeped in anti-Communism the nation's Self-Defense Forces are. A Communist Party official and four other civilians who were members of the Japan-China Friendship Association visited a Self-Defense Force base in Okayama Prefecture, in western Japan, in August 1971. Suddenly nineteen SDF men, including a lieutenant colonel, fell upon the visitors, hitting them with their fists and heaping insults on them, calling them "traitors" and "damned fools." The incident evoked memories of the prewar period when many citizens, not only Communists, were assaulted on suspicion of having liberal ideas concerning politics.

7

Reinterpreting the Past

At the crematory, thirteen pieces of a mortar projectile, which had rested in my father's flesh and pained him severely during his life, were found among his ashes.

> —From a statement by a sixteen-year-old Japanese high-school girl (1969)

If that was "imperialism," then it was glorious imperialism.

> —Foreign Minister Etsusaburo Shiina, in remarks made to the Diet in 1966 in defense of Japan's wartime policy

In mid-1971 a most intriguing speech, touching on lessons gained from World War II, was made before the America-Japan Society in Tokyo by one of Japan's most nimble and influential politicians. Yasuhiro Nakasone, an early advocate of rearmament, told his audience that Japan's diplomacy should henceforth rest on four principles:

1. Japan must do nothing beyond its national strength.
2. Japan must take no gambler's risks.
3. Japan must have a reliable ally.
4. Japan must not be isolated from world currents.

Five years before, the last will, or testament, of wartime Premier-General Hideki Tojo had been unearthed. It also made reference to the lessons Japan learned from the war.

Here is Tojo's brief document, purported to be authentic, in its entirety:

To the peoples of Britain and the United States:

Japan lost the war because of lack of power. I admit this, but I must censure you for killing so many innocent noncombatants, both men and women, with atomic bombs.

To the people of Japan:

Japan was defeated because of lack of power. It must be remembered, however, that this divine country is immortal. Japan should rise up again in the future.

To all youths:

A right and just country does not always prove a winner in war and Japan lost the war because of lack of power. You must never be desperate; you must realize that the future of this country rests on your shoulders. Be diligent!

Tojo's statement clearly shows that the wartime leader is, perhaps naturally, not even disposed to hint at Japanese culpability. There is not a word of remorse; instead, there is a litany of power. There is the counsel against impulsiveness. Nakasone, in his speech, warned against gambling. Are the lessons drawn by these two men so different?

How Tojo's last testament was found remains a puzzle. His widow said the document was genuine and had been written shortly before Tojo shot himself in an attempted suicide on September 11, 1945. He went to the gallows as a war criminal in 1948. The contents were made public in 1966 by Ichiro Kiyose, a well-known ruling-party leader and archconservative, now deceased. Kiyose said he obtained the document from a high-school teacher.

Forbidden to hold office at the war's end, Kiyose nonetheless helped defend Tojo at the International Military Tribunal for the Far East. So it may be presumed that Kiyose, who supported many right-wing causes during his lifetime, had a personal interest in exonerating the fallen Tojo.

But it was not the first time efforts were made to rebuild Tojo's image. A few years ago, an ultrarightist memorial to Tojo was unveiled near Mt. Fuji, a noble mountain with a religious symbolism for many Japanese. Many religious groups have their head temples located near Fuji.*

In the middle 1960's, when many democratic reforms made in the early postwar years under the U.S. Occupation were under pressure from the ultranationalists, a photo-

---

* The Tojo memorial was damaged by a bomb explosion in December 1971, apparently set off by radical leftists in revenge for the mutilation of a statue of a Socialist leader by ultrarightists.

graph of a benign and paternal Tojo, in military uniform, suddenly appeared in a new primary-school textbook.

Was it a trial balloon to test the public's reaction? Naturally, there was strong opposition from liberal teachers, parents, and left-wing political parties, and the photo was later removed. But many other photographs, which had previously been in the schoolbooks and had depicted the misery and futility of militarism and war, have been deleted one after another, as if by calculation. Such photos have not been replaced, although a few mild protests have been made about their disappearance.

Whether or not there is a direct connection between these deleted photographs and the tendency of mass culture to glorify war and violence, a prominent politician, former Foreign Minister Aiichiro Fujiyama, has assailed the habit of Japanese youths to romanticize war and bloodshed.

Education Ministry officials have also removed from schoolbooks all photographs of the atomic mushroom cloud, of Hiroshima's famed atomic-dome memorial, of Japanese women during the war dressed in *mompe* (baggy trousers) and lined up to get potato and cereal rations, of people evacuating the cities, and of the war crimes trials.

Moreover, passages about old warrior heroes and stories of the mythical foundations of the Japanese Empire have been revived or lengthened. By contrast, in some geography texts where there were formerly several pages devoted to China, the information has been pared to a few paragraphs.

A concerted drive is under way to resurrect many of the old loyalties, to describe, and circumscribe, the ideal Japanese, and to change the people's thinking about the war and military matters in general.

There has been a campaign, led by right-wing intellectuals, to vindicate Japan's role in the war on the grounds that this role was indispensable from the viewpoint of the destiny of the nation. Of course, other nations, too, have been reappraising World War II for many years. For example, some American intellectuals, after re-examining the origins of the Pacific War, have directed much of the blame at shortsighted American policies.

Each year, exhibitions are held at major department stores in big and small cities. These exhibits display war memorabilia, such as Japanese military uniforms and armaments, and paintings of the war. Often, such displays are supported by the Defense Agency and veterans' groups.

Since the early 1960's the Japanese government has awarded posthumous decorations to the war dead, both military and civilian. In November 1971, the total number of decorated was 1,945,502. In addition, 71,056 had received honorific court ranks.

Those decorated include not only men who perished in the Sino-Japanese War that began in the early 1930's but also Okinawan nurses and schoolgirls, some of whom killed themselves, either voluntarily, to prevent capture, or at the orders of the Japanese Army, to spare more food for the soldiers. Among those posthumously decorated were Admiral Chuichi Nagumo, who directed the attack on Pearl Harbor in 1941 and lost his life during the battle of Midway, and Gotaro Ogawa, who was supreme adviser to the Imperial Army.

Meanwhile, government missions have been going out to the far-flung islands of the Pacific where the battles were fought to collect the remains of scores of thousands of Japanese soldiers.

There is a campaign to erase the words from the Hiroshima cenotaph which read: "Rest Ye in Peace, for the

Error Shall Not Be Repeated." The campaign is led by Yoshio Kodama.

Kodama, who has been an adviser and financial backer to the ruling party, attained questionable fame in 1970 when he composed a racial song evoking memories of Nazi Party rallying songs of World War II. Kodama titled his song, *Minzoku no Uta* ("The Song of the Race") and it was first performed publicly at Tokyo's plush Okura Hotel before three thousand eminent guests, including former Prime Minister Nobusuke Kishi and industrial and political leaders. "The Song of the Race" cries out for revival of the kamikaze attack spirit, including absolute devotion to the state and a willingness to die for a racial-nationalist goal. American journalist David Conde describes the song as one "seeking restoration of power to the Emperor with its intimation of a militarily achieved nationalism-socialism accomplished at gun-point in a *coup d'état,* all reeking with racism."

After studying Japanese life for over ten years, Dr. F. Kenneth Berrien, a social psychologist at Rutgers University in New Jersey, offers this conclusion: "Japanese society shows strong signs of reversion to many of its original characteristics as an autocratic society." The survey, sponsored by the United States Navy, was completed in 1969 and confirms this author's observations about the anachronisms prevalent in Japanese society. Dr. Berrien and his team of researchers reported that many rural communities were undemocratically run. Leaders were invariably chosen not for their talents but because of their power and influence.

As noted, there is in Japanese society a continuing emphasis on the martial arts, which have a close association with the iron discipline of the warrior. In schools and universities as well as neighborhood clubs, such sports as judo, kendo, and karate are widely practiced and beatings and hazings are common, resulting in a number of deaths each year. Some deaths at the hands of sadistic sportsmen are reported as accidents.

A favorite form of punishment—it is called "teaching discipline"—is to beat a victim's body with bamboo sticks or bamboo swords. Reports of such beatings are legion. At Nihon University's boxing club, six junior members were beaten so severely with bamboo swords in July 1971 that they required medical treatment. The beatings were a regular part of training.

A poll taken among the 8,241 students at Takushoku University in 1970 showed one of every five students had suffered some form of violence or intimidation from members of martial-arts clubs. The president of Takushoku at that time was Yasuhiro Nakasone, a ranking member of the nation's ruling party, who remains an official at the school.

After World War II, the martial arts were ordered de-emphasized, and all films and dramas that extolled war or violence were banned. The most popular vendetta drama in all Japan—*Chusingura*—as well as other works with a revenge motif or filled with excessive sword play, were taboo because they helped perpetuate the feudalistic way of thinking which condoned violence.

Nevertheless, these works represent very heroic drama, and the Japanese can see many versions of *Chusingura* at present on television or in the theater. The drama is about forty-seven *ronin,* or masterless samurai, who avenge their lord. Afterwards all are ordered to kill themselves by their own hands. The event actually occurred early in the eighteenth century, and the tombs of the forty-seven ronin, ranging in age from fifteen to seventy-seven, are situated inside a Tokyo temple. Tales such as this help to inspire loyalty, honor, and obedience in the people.

Also making a comeback after being outlawed by the U.S. Occupation is *kigensetsu,* or National Foundation Day. This day is based on the legendary accession to the throne of Japan's first Emperor, Jimmu, more than twenty-six centuries ago. Despite protests from scientists, teachers, writers, artists, liberal politicians, and others, the government and ruling party restored kigensetsu as a national holiday in 1966. They were backed by the efforts of the right wing and the National Association of Shinto Shrines.

There is also a gathering momentum to nationalize certain memorials and to give state support and money to religious shrines, such as Yasukuni Shrine in Tokyo. This is a famous Shinto shrine dedicated to the nation's war dead. But since state support would appear to challenge the separation of church and state, which is written into the Constitution, the ruling party has searched for ways to get by this ban. A possible maneuver would be to turn Yasukuni into a nonreligious shrine.

Much of this may be the normal reaction of a country that was occupied and is returning to its own traditions. But the Japanese scene has some features that cause uneasiness. There seems to be a pattern to the attacks on the new democratic thinking of the postwar era. Many memorials have to do with war or war heroes. On entering shrines, you sometimes see a very old and formidable-looking cannon staring you in the face.

Yasukuni is, in large measure, a military shrine. In wartime, before young kamikaze pilots took off on their suicide missions, they sometimes consoled each other with the parting words: "I'll meet you at Yasukuni!" These fallen warriors are now enshrined there.

In addition, what causes misgivings among many Japanese is that in deciding issues of social importance, such as the establishment of National Foundation Day and the adoption of laws for university reform, the popular will is often ignored. The opinions of the nation's intelligentsia, including Japan's two Nobel Prize-winning scientists, Hideki Yukawa and Shinichiro Tomonaga, as well as teachers, artists, and critics, are generally overlooked. On the other hand, the shrine associations, the veterans' organizations, the most conservative politicians, and the patriotic societies often get their way in these matters. In a word, these are generally the very groups who avidly support rearmament and a revival of the former pattern of living.

Shortly after the U.S. Occupation ended, those statues or memorials that had been banned were either rebuilt or taken out of mothballs. For example, after seventeen years of retirement, the mounted statue of Field Marshal Iwao Oyama found its final resting place at the Yasukuni Shrine. In 1947 the U.S. Occupation authorities ordered its removal from its location in front of the old General Staff Headquarters. Oyama was a hero of the Sino-Japanese and Russo-Japanese wars who died in 1916.

The flagship of Admiral Heihachiro Togo, the *Mikasa,* was rebuilt and turned into a national memorial at Yokosuka, near Tokyo. Togo won lasting fame for destroying the Imperial Russian fleet in the 1905 battle of Tsushima Straits.

After its reconstruction, which was aided by contributions from many U.S. Navy officers and men, Shinzo Koizumi, a member of the Japan Academy, called on the nation, "particularly young boys and girls, to visit this memorial and, while thinking of Japan's past, present, and future, renew in their hearts the feeling of self-respect and self-reliance along with self-reflection." Koizumi said he wanted the story of the great sea battle, which set the militarist tone of the 1920's and 1930's, to be passed on from father to son and its great significance recalled every year.

Following Japan's brilliant victory over czarist Russia, the world began to show interest in Bushido, the Japanese martial code, and to be apprehensive about its application.

A British journalist, Alfred Stead, wrote perceptively in 1906:

We recognize grudgingly and in spite of ourselves the existence of a moral force that appears to be able to govern and sway the whole conduct of a whole people, inspiring not a caste, but a nation, from highest to lowest, to deeds that are worthy to rank with the most famous of history or legend. . . . We want to know what this force is, whence it comes, and what it means; the sense of its existence makes us jealous, uncomfortable, almost annoyed.

Stead wondered whether Japan might abuse the power it was building up rapidly.

In the mid-1960's the government made an effort to define the so-called ideal Japanese. Before the war, various official or quasi-official definitions existed of the ideal Japanese—the most loyal citizen. Behind the concept was the subtle attempt to promote thought control among the population; by and large, the attempt was quite successful.

The Education Ministry, in 1965, prepared a long interim report, composed of 18,000 ideographs, on the ideal

Japanese. The report concluded that a spiritual vacuum existed in postwar Japan and that there was a need to foster nationalism and promote respect for the Emperor, the flag, and the national anthem.

Here is part of the introduction:

We have carried the flag and sung the anthem and loved and revered the Emperor as symbols of Japan. This was not apart from our loving Japan and paying respect to her mission. The Emperor is a symbol of Japan and of the unity of the people. We must give our deep thought to the fact that our loving and revering our fatherland, Japan, is identical with loving and revering the Emperor.

Probably, the authors of the document did not intend a revival of the cult of the Emperor. Before the war, such a cult was used as an auxiliary to militarism and to stress Japan's superiority over other nations. However, the ruling party is striving to elevate the Emperor's status at the present time.

By way of comparison, here is a portion of the 1941 report, "Way of Subjects," issued by the Education Ministry:

However diverse the Empire's structures in politics, economy, culture, military affairs, and others, may be, all finally are unified under the Emperor, the center. The subjects of the Emperor, with one mind, fulfill their way of loyalty and filial piety and support the Imperial tasks. The fundamental character of Japan, invariable forever and ever, is glorified in this.

Naturally, there was keen opposition to the 1965 report. To many intellectuals and liberals, it seemed that each point raised in the report on the ideal Japanese indicated a secret desire by the authorities to curtail democratic rights guaranteed in the postwar Constitution.

Also, these critics were alarmed because the report largely disregarded the postwar stress on individuality and personality. This stress, of course, was a reaction against the abject obedience of citizens to the former militarist regime. In addition, the report was attacked for its vigorous support of nationalism. During World War II, it was nationalism, Shintoism (which was synonymous with Emperor worship), and militarism that were, so to speak, the glue holding the Empire together.

Under such conditions, a free press was an impossibility. If an editor tried to preserve his integrity, he was the target of malevolent criticism as well as intimidation. To suppress one brave editor, army warplanes dived on the newspaper offices of the *Nichinichi Shimbun* in Fukuoka in May 1932, terrorizing the entire staff. Rokko Kikutake, the paper's chief editorial writer, had forthrightly condemned the militarists and ultranationalists for murdering Prime Minister Tsuyoshi Inukai in the so-called Five-Fifteen Incident of May 15, 1932. Militarists, wrote the editor, were striving to popularize Fascism.

Before the mock bombing of the newspaper, army officers made dozens of threats against the paper and its staff. A leader of the army faction making the most threats against the paper was the commanding officer of the Fukuoka prefectural garrison at that time. His name was Hideki Tojo.

Professor Tatsukichi Minobe, father of the incumbent Governor of Tokyo, propounded an influential theory which said the Emperor's sovereignty existed because he was the highest organ of the state. In 1935 his books were banned and he had to resgin his teaching post. Most of the newspapers and academic circles were afraid to speak out in his defense, although many secretly agreed with his ideas.

The postwar record of brute force used against the mass media is hardly reassuring. In 1961 a band of ultrarightists and gangster elements raided the mass-circulation *Mainichi Shimbun,* throwing sand into the presses and delaying publication. The attackers said they were taking revenge for the paper's criticism of their organization. In 1968 a dozen right-wing ultranationalists entered the studios of Nippon Educational Television in Tokyo, and harassed a producer for an hour. They claimed that his program on *Kimigayo,* the national anthem, was slanted to the left. Dozens of threatening phone calls also were received by the station.

More serious was a plot discovered by police in August 1971 to blow up the *Asahi Shimbun* building, located in the heart of Tokyo. Police arrested a trio of rightist extremists who had 225 sticks of dynamite in their possession. Under questioning, one of the three said that the mass communications media was "leaning too much toward the left," and therefore, "we thought of blowing up the *Asahi* as a warning."

Curiously, these two giant papers, *Asahi* and *Mainichi,* took an early critical stance toward the American involvement in Indochina, and both were sharply assailed by the U.S. State Department for alleged pro-Communism.

The unmistakable right-wing trend of Japanese society is perhaps nowhere better illustrated than in the battle of the textbooks.

A few years ago, the mythology surrounding Japan's earliest history was accompanied by a warning in schoolbooks that these classic legends were not necessarily historical truths. Now many of these warnings to young readers have disappeared. An example is the story of the descent to earth of the sun goddess, Amaterasu, whose direct descendants supposedly founded the Japanese nation. This legend is now back in the textbooks. Such myths were banned right after World War II when the Emperor renounced his divine status.

For over a decade a textbook dispute has been waged in the courts, and it goes on, even though the plaintiffs, a liberal scholar and his backers, have managed to win a battle or two in the lower courts. The basic problem is that liberal intellectuals who write history use the strict criteria of scholarship and are likely to clash directly with government views as to how history should be presented. This clash includes the presentation of traditional mythology.

The difficulty is sharpened by the racial and chauvinist overtones prevalent in Japanese history. There seems to be a rising trend toward ethnocentrism or, as author-editor Kiyoaki Murata has expressed it, "mythical nationalism." Japan, too, has its racist historians. One of them, Jiro Murau, has written a book on Japan entitled *Racial Flow in Life,* in which the author urges revival of all classic myths about Japan's divine origins as traditionally taught in the schools.*

It is instructive to illustrate some of the changes found in the new textbooks. An early postwar text said: "A tie was affected among the Fascist capitals of Berlin, Rome, and Tokyo." A new text says: "Berlin, Rome, and Tokyo were linked up with each other." An earlier text said: "As rearmament advanced [in the postwar period], opinions opposing it and wanting to protect the Constitution became stronger." This has been cut entirely from a revised

---

* This gentleman is in charge of checking textbooks for the Education Ministry.

edition, which gives a terse explanation of the origin of the new military forces in Japan.

A new account of the origins of World War II is especially revealing. Here is the account as it appeared in a 1954 text:

Although Japan won the war against China on the battlefield, it failed to achieve its original aim to rule China. The Chinese did their best in resisting the Japanese troops. . . . As Japan faced a deadlock in fighting against China and became unsure of when and how to end the war, the Japanese people's anxiety and dissatisfaction began to surge up. The Japanese market in China didn't expand as Japan had expected. Because of the economic pressure of the United States and Great Britain, Japan faced problems in obtaining raw materials and felt it necessary to open new markets in Southeast Asian areas. Then World War II broke out. . . . Using this opportunity, Japan sent its troops into French Indochina in 1940. America and Great Britain tried to restrict Japan's expansion in Southeast Asia by banning exports of iron and oil to Japan. Relations between the United States and Japan worsened day by day. . . .

And a 1970 text reads:

Japan considered that the reason why the China Incident could not be settled easily was that the United States, Great Britain, and France were helping China by giving material aid. So Japan thought it should cut such aid, liberate Southeast Asian areas from Western colonial rule, establish and lead the Greater East Asia Co-prosperity Sphere and use at will raw materials of those areas. Japan took advantage of the fact that Germany defeated France in 1940, and upon concluding an agreement with France, it sent its troops to northern French Indochina and, later, southern Indochina. In view of this situation, the United States restricted its oil and iron exports to Japan, thus worsening the relationship of the two nations. Great Britain and Holland, which owned colonies in Southeast Asia, began to put pressure on Japan, too.

In short, the new version is a justification for Japanese entry into French Indochina. Also, the term "Greater East Asia Co-prosperity Sphere" makes its appearance. This term helped make the aims of Japanese conquest more palatable to the Japanese people by reassuring many who were not at all enthusiastic about the war.

In view of such alterations, it is not surprising to find protests even from students. A junior-high-school girl from Sendai, north of Tokyo, recently wrote a letter to a major newspaper in which she objected to the fact that photographs showing a loyalty oath being signed by factory girls and events of the anti-Japanese movement in wartime China which appeared in the textbook she used in 1969 (". . . and which particularly impressed me") would not be included in the revised text.

The girl, Keiko Homma, added: "Those were the pictures that made me understand the other side of Japan, which I had not known." Commenting on the excision of these "valuable documentary pictures," she said: "Our teacher told us that Prime Minister Tojo and others were sentenced to death at trials. I was also told that those who committed major war crimes were duly punished. I cannot help thinking that the Education Ministry hates the darkness of war."

She ended her letter with the question: "Can we be allowed to grow up without knowing the horrors of war?"

8

The Endangered Constitution

Aspiring sincerely to an international peace based on justice and order, the Japanese people forever renounce war as a sovereign right of the nation and the threat or use of force as means of settling international disputes.

In order to accomplish the aim of the preceding paragraph, land, sea, and air forces, as well as other war potential, will never be maintained. The right of belligerency of the state will not be recognized.

—Article 9, the Japanese Constitution, 1947

I have staked my political career on a revision of the Constitution of Japan.

—Former Prime Minister Nobusuke Kishi, at an anti-Communist rally in Manila, 1971

I will devote the rest of my life to lobbying for an American constitutional amendment patterned after Japan's Article 9 (the famed pacifist clause).

—Dr. Robert M. Hutchins, educator and former president of University of Chicago, in a statement made in 1965

The Japanese government and ruling party are coolly plotting to undo the peace Constitution before the end of the decade. But they have run into a formidable snag: the people are not yet convinced the nation needs a new law, and they are suspicious of maneuvers to alter the basic document, which many regard as a last dike against a new wave of militarism and Fascism in Japan.

Since the Constitution may not be legally rejected without the people's consent by special election or referendum, government leaders acknowledge the present time is not ripe for change.

But politician Yasuhiro Nakasone, whose name crops up often, thinks 1975 is a good date for sealing the matter. Why 1975? Because, he says, thirty years after the end of the Pacific War is a good time to rid the nation of its Constitution, which was born under alien auspices. Like other revisionists, Nakasone regards the 1947 charter as a foreign, or translated document, not in keeping with present realities.

The revisionists, however, are not impatient. For while the peace Constitution remains, the government is able to use it to counter rising charges of militaristic revival. The revisionists ask the question: "How can anyone call Japan 'militaristic' when it has a pacifist Constitution?"

Nevertheless, many persons are alarmed at the preparations being made to overturn this Constitution.

The ruling party has already drawn up a number of preliminary drafts for a new charter, which include a wholly new Article 9, the famed antiwar mainstay. That article forbids possession of full-fledged armed forces. These drafts not only clarify the legality of the Self-Defense Forces but allow dispatch of these forces overseas in certain cases. One such case would be to help with peace-keeping duties in world trouble spots.

Moreover, for many years the ruling party has had one committee or another, including a special nonpartisan group, study the feasibility of revising the postwar Constitution. Since those against revision usually avoid such committees, the emphasis of the committees is naturally weighted in favor of changing the Constitution.

What many people worry about is whether the revisionists have ulterior motives in pressing for a change in the Constitution. Even Okinori Kaya, one of the ruling party's right-wing theorists and an elder statesman, says candidly a nation can be two-faced: "A nation which is actually intent on aggression can pretend it supports a policy of peace and coexistence." But Japan will never be such a nation again, Kaya and other leaders say positively.

Observers point out that at the height of Japanese aggression in the 1930's and early 1940's, the militarists and jingo plutocrats always maintained that Japan was bent on keeping the peace and that it was fighting only to suppress warlike elements, including bandits.

Thus, in October 1971, grave suspicions were aroused among all the opposition parties and among many scholars, intellectuals, and newspapers when the Defense Agency director general proposed that Japan's Self-Defense Forces might be sent abroad as part of relief and natural-disaster teams. It was a curious proposal which was unimportant in itself. However, coupled with a trend in the ruling party to push the nation further to the right and to strengthen Japan's ties with other anti-Communist states, the proposal takes on added significance.

Learning of the proposal, a young Japanese administrator in Tokyo exclaimed in my presence, "Oh, oh, here it comes!"

The revisionists say that although Article 9 must be revoked, the pacifist spirit of the charter will still stay. But since Article 9 is the core of pacifism in the document, critics regard such an argument as specious.

Dr. Yoshikazu Sakamoto, a legal expert at Tokyo University, noting that even the zaibatsu are urging removal of Article 9, says: "There is no doubt that the enthusiastic call for revision of war-renouncing Article 9 of the Constitution by some business and financial leaders here in Japan has raised suspicion as to the destination of Japan's high economic growth."

Indeed, the powerful *Nikkeiren* (Japan Federation of Employers' Associations), in which the zaibatsu is influential, has unabashedly said that Article 9 poses an obstacle to future Japanese efforts to promote collective security in Asia.

A main part of the controversy centering on the Constitution is whether the Self-Defense Forces are legal or not. The ruling-party line is probably shown in the following incident.

Yasuhiro Nakasone, giving testimony in December 1971 at the Tokyo District Court where three followers of Yukio Mishima who took part in the Mishima Incident were being tried, said he believed the SDF were Constitutional. But he reiterated his own view that the Supreme Court should make clear its stand concerning the opposite view—that the SDF are unlawful.

Indeed, even if the Supreme Court finally declared that

the defense forces are absolutely legal, the words contained in Article 9 would remain to haunt the courts and the government.

Despite this article, the SDF not only exists but its armament is expanding rapidly. One may, therefore, wonder, since the charter is really so elastic, why any revision is thought necessary. The answer is that, in addition to wanting Article 9 thrown out, the ruling party is seeking other major alterations.

In the drafts for a new charter, basic democratic ideas either are missing or are watered down considerably. Rights of individuals are curtailed, and the national interests are stressed.

Also, and this causes much apprehension, parts of the antiquated Meiji Constitution (1889–1945), as well as laws of the Meiji era, are incorporated into the drafts: for example, the loyalties of the old family system are clearly defined.

Furthermore, the Emperor, who is now a symbol of the nation, "deriving his position from the will of the people," is elevated to head of the state. This raises fears of a return to the prewar model whereby the militarist clique made cunning use of the Emperor's name and position.

Of course, elevation of the Emperor's status is a major plank of every ultranationalist program. All are demanding a *Showa* Restoration—Showa being the name of Hirohito's reign.

The softening-up process preparatory to actual Constitutional revision involves fiery speeches by everybody from Cabinet ministers to right-wing intellectuals who want an independent Constitution for an independent nation.

Increasingly, one sees sound trucks, advertisements, and handbills being used to urge revision of the charter. There is an organized campaign involving young men, dressed in white uniforms with white baseball caps, which asks the people to think hard about the alien origins of the Constitution.

Among the most zealous supporters of revision are Nobusuke Kishi and Okinori Kaya. In numerous speeches, Kishi's words have had an ultranationalistic ring. He deplores the decline of the nation's postwar morality. For this, he blames the Constitution. He also blames it for contributing to the increase of Communists in Japan. He once said that "the selfish acts of individual persons and groups you see today derive from the conflicting aspects of the Constitution."

The former Prime Minister, in his speeches, favors expressions like *Yamato Damashii* ("the Japanese spirit") and the "Greater East-Asia Co-prosperity Sphere." The latter slogan is, of course, closely associated with militarism. In addition, Kishi supports a big military build-up, and he has come out strongly for Japanese possession of nuclear arms.

The revisionists underline the foreign origin of the Constitution. It should be noted that many of the Japanese who were asked to help frame the first postwar Constitution in 1945 and 1946 were not in favor of making radical changes from the old Meiji charter. Therefore, the U.S. Occupation authorities stepped in and ordered democratic clauses inserted into the new document.

Yet, for all its pacifist ideology, the Constitution proved to be quite flexible for proponents of rearmament. Even General MacArthur showed how loosely it could be interpreted. Early in 1950, MacArthur told the Japanese people that "by no sophistry of reasoning" could Article 9 be seen as a complete denial of the right of self-defense.

America had its reasons. It wished to make Japan a dependable ally against Communism, especially after the Korean War started. The United States discovered, too, that those most useful in this struggle were by and large the very men MacArthur's command had purged because of their militaristic or ultranationalistic leanings. They were reinstated, and many of them naturally clambered back into political power.

Thoughtful Japanese, who had welcomed the new democratic Constitution, were amazed to see the quick rehabilitation of the Old Guard.

Meanwhile, there was a steady influx of American scholars, politicians, and businessmen into Japan. Many came to coax Japan to rearm and even to urge the Japanese to rewrite the very Constitution which the Americans had helped inspire. One U.S. Congressman bluntly asked the State Department to put pressure on Japan to change its Constitution in order that Japan's military build-up could proceed more quickly. That was in 1969.

Richard M. Nixon came on the scene much earlier, in 1953, arriving in Japan as Vice President. He immediately stunned the Japanese nation by saying that America had blundered in 1947 by insisting on Article 9. Japan, he hinted, could rectify the error by changing the charter. For its part, America would have no objection.

From Washington's viewpoint, the Korean War had proved the enormous value of the military alliance with Japan, under which Japan permitted American bases on its soil. Without such bases, the U.S. strategy in Korea would have been difficult to carry out.

Japan accepted its first Constitution in 1889 as a gift from Emperor Meiji, who had sought enlightenment from Europe and America in order to make Japan a powerful and modern industrial nation. At that time, all Japan rejoiced.

Onto this scene came British author and poet Rudyard Kipling, who recorded that he was startled when the first Japanese he encountered thrust a copy of the new charter into his hands, saying with evident rapture: "The Emperor Meiji made it himself."

But although the people were excited, the new Constitution gave them few favors. It was a document in which democratic ideas were conspicuously absent. All power reposed in the throne. Nevertheless, it was Japan's first Constitution.

It was nostalgia for the Meiji era and for Japan's martial past that overwhelmed Yukio Mishima, who, before his suicide, railed against the peace Constitution in the most frenzied terms. His zeal is shown by the question he asked: "Is there no one who will die by hurling his body against the Constitution which has mutilated Japan?"

Later, Mishima's disciples emulated his fury. In the courtroom where survivors of the Mishima Incident were being tried, one young follower said: "We decided to kill the Constitution in exchange for our lives because we could not tolerate it any longer."

The government and ruling party acknowledge it will be some time before they can tackle revision through parliamentary means, which involves obtaining a majority in both houses plus ratification by the people. But there is always the danger that the Constitution will be suspended through a successful *coup d'état*.

However, despite the frustrations of the military over their legitimacy, such extralegal action probably will not occur under present conditions. Meddling by the military in politics does not appear to be a present danger, although it is widely believed that the Self-Defense Forces would not sit idly by if the left-wing parties were about to form a coalition government after having won a majority of seats in the National Diet.

Yet now and then a disturbing incident occurs. A few years ago, some young officers who called themselves the Second Lieutenants Group wrote a stinging letter to leading members of the ruling Liberal-Democratic Party. The officers attacked the alleged peace mood of the government and demanded repeal of the Constitution.

The letter, according to insiders, sent chills down the spines of those who read it. This was natural; it evoked the 1930's when bands of young mutinous officers attempted to overthrow the civilian governments.

But perhaps more disturbing than the actual content of the letter was that neither the government nor the ruling party nor the Defense Agency, as far as could be determined, took any action to reprimand those officers who wrote it.

9

Japan, China, and Taiwan

Is it not that some people in Japan are still thinking that Taiwan is a special area just as in the past? It also seems that Japan is taking part in the U.S. Seventh Fleet's control of Taiwan.

  —Prime Minister Chou En-lai, interview with Japanese delegation, 1971

Japan has been the latest, most formidable, and most devastating of all China's foreign invaders since the Opium War of 1840. The events of 1931–45 are bound to have left a legacy of resentment and suspicion in Chinese minds.

  —Arnold Toynbee, in 1968 article for *Mainichi* Newspapers

The mayor of Taipei, Henry Y. S. Kao, was speaking candidly to me about his fears for the future of Taiwan, where he was born (the Portuguese called it *Ilha Formosa* or "beautiful island"). I had tossed a formidable question at him: Was he more worried about an invasion from China or a takeover by Japan? Without hesitation, this soft-spoken, Japan-educated engineer and civic leader, replied: "Of course, Japan. . . ."

His reply was startling. Japan, he said, wanted eventually to control Taiwan. He actually used the verb "to annex." A subtropical island, Taiwan was a valuable Japanese property for half a century, economically and strategically, until 1945, when the colony reverted to Kuomintang (Nationalist Chinese) rule.*

Here was the anti-Communist mayor of Taiwan's capital (estimated population in 1972: 1.7 million) in apparent full agreement with Chinese Prime Minister Chou En-lai concerning alleged Japanese militaristic ambitions for Taiwan. Kao fairly warmed up to the subject. I had known him and his charming physician-wife ten years before when I worked on Taiwan as Bureau Manager for United Press International. So I was delighted when he telephoned in the summer of 1971 and invited me to his suite at Tokyo's Imperial Hotel, where he and his wife were stopping for a few days. Speaking in fluent English, the mayor con-

---

* To allay any misunderstanding, I wish to make it clear that Mayor Kao, who was appointed Minister of Communications in mid-1972, is not anti-Japanese. In fact, some of his strongest ties are with Japan.

tinued: "First, the Japanese will dominate Taiwan economically. Already, Japanese investments and industry are considerable and are expanding. Second, they will control the island politically, and third, the military will arrive. Japan will try to annex Taiwan. Wait and see!"

So far, the most troubled with Japan's real or alleged ambitions for Taiwan has been the Peking regime. Chou En-lai has recently accused Japan of plotting with Kuomintang leaders to create an independent Taiwan; that is, the establishment of a non-Chinese government on the island, at least in name. It is hard to prove such accusations. But certain factors stand out.

Japan's role in Taiwan's economy is impressive. Forty-five major Japanese industries have formed joint ventures on the island, including many zaibatsu. In December 1971, Japanese firms had invested approximately $150 million in 391 projects on Taiwan. Total foreign investment in Taiwan was about half a billion dollars, with America's share around $200 million. But this was said to be tapering off. Of over five hundred factories built by foreign capital between 1953 and 1970, more than three hundred were at least partly Japanese-owned. Japanese firms virtually monopolized the Taiwan market in such items as pharmaceuticals, farm machines, man-made fibers, and electronic equipment. As *Fortune* magazine said in November 1971, Japan has "an enormous stake in Taiwan's economy."

In addition to investments, *Fortune* said: "The long years of Japanese rule left firm, continuing ties with the dominant Taiwanese commercial groups. Giant trading companies in Tokyo finance many of these businessmen and in turn handle *nearly half of Taiwan's two-way trade*." [Italics added.] The magazine also said Japan's net trade surplus from all this totaled $364,500,000 in 1970.

It may be only natural that Japan, with its strong commercial links to Taiwan, should seek every means to safeguard and expand these links. Everyone in Japan knows that the zaikai, the most powerful financial and industrial leaders, not only run the nation's economy but also have the power of life and death over the Prime Minister and his Cabinet. Zaibatsu industrialists have declared that whoever controls Taiwan controls the sea lanes from the South China Sea to Japan, which pass close to Taiwan. It is a related sister theory to the Malacca Strait Defense Line mentioned earlier. The right wing, or mainstream of the ruling party, holds that a Communist regime on Taiwan would be intolerable. Okinori Kaya, a senior party leader on the right, says that Japan's national interests demand a non-Communist flag on the island. Obviously, most politicians belonging to the Kuomintang avidly support such concepts because they contribute nicely to their own survival.

Such views seem related to the somewhat dated idea of containing China as well as to the security treaty linking Japan and America.

In many ways, the United States helped stage-manage Japan's China policy in the postwar years. Of course, this is no longer true. Japan was angry and humiliated over the Nixon visit to Peking in 1972 largely because the Americans did not consult Tokyo beforehand. Previously, U.S. policy not only kept America's contacts with China to a minimum but also did much to inhibit Japanese association with the mainland. Naturally, the 13 million people on Taiwan had no communication with China.

Along with the Nixon doctrine of having Asians gradually help themselves and defend themselves, the U.S. government in 1969 virtually recognized Japan's sphere of influence in Taiwan when the American President signed a communiqué with Prime Minister Sato in which Japan said that Taiwan was an important factor in its security. Peking, suspecting the worst, accused Japan of having ulterior designs on Taiwan.

The Tokyo government has provided China with additional grounds for worry. In the past, Japanese officials have questioned the legal title to Taiwan, which has provoked the wrath of Peking's leaders. Meanwhile, Japan has laid claim to the Senkaku (Tiaoyu) Islands, which lie midway between Okinawa and Taiwan. But both Taiwan and the Senkakus have always been Chinese soil according to Peking.

Thus there has arisen another quarrelsome issue between the two neighbors. Peking sees the Japanese claim as "proof" of militarism. But the Japanese are not about to surrender their claim, although they would like to settle the dispute, if possible, through talks.

Everyone interested in the future of Taiwan ought to note what the Nixon-Chou communiqué issued in Shanghai on February 27, 1972, said about this problem. The Chinese side said:

The Taiwan question is the crucial question obstructing the normalization of relations between China and the United States; the government of the People's Republic of China is the sole legal government of China; Taiwan is a province of China which has long been returned to the motherland; the liberation of Taiwan is China's internal affair in which no other country has the right to interfere; and all U.S. forces and military installations must be withdrawn from Taiwan. The Chinese government firmly opposes any activities which aim at the creation of "one China, one Taiwan," "one China, two governments," "two Chinas" and "Independent Taiwan" or advocate that "the status of Taiwan remains to be determined."

The U.S. side said:

The United States acknowledges that all Chinese on either side of the Taiwan Strait maintain there is but one China and that Taiwan is a part of China. The United States government does not challenge that position. It reaffirms its interest in a peaceful settlement of the Taiwan question by the Chinese themselves. With this prospect in mind, it affirms the ultimate objective of the withdrawal of all U.S. forces and military installations from Taiwan. In the meantime, it will progressively reduce its forces and military installations on Taiwan as the tension in the area diminishes.

China omitted any mention of Japan in connection with the Taiwan problem, although it has often singled out Japan for abuse on this issue. (The Shanghai communiqué said separately that China "firmly opposes the revival and outward expansion of Japanese militarism and firmly supports the Japanese people's desire to build an independent, democratic, peaceful and neutral Japan.")

Japan has actually been so absorbed in the problem of Taiwan that even foreign statesmen like Georges Pompidou have commented on it. A few years before he became President of France, Pompidou, after meeting with Japanese officials, pointed out that Japan was showing extraordinary interest in the disposition of Taiwan. But the Tokyo government is not the only group in Japan that is interested in the problem. In 1971, the ultrarightist camp demonstrated more than usual concern with Taiwan. For instance, Ryoichi Sasagawa, a leading nationalist, went to Taiwan with other ultrarightists, and conferred with top Nationalist Chinese officials. Sasagawa, who openly calls for Taiwan's independence, is reported to have close ties with the mainstream of the Japanese ruling party.

Thousands of Taiwanese expatriates are living in Japan who actively campaign for Taiwan's independence. They complain that although many major powers talk of self-determination for all peoples, the wishes of Taiwan's citizens as to what government they want have never been taken into account.

These Taiwanese formerly held Nationalist Chinese passports, many now expired. Nevertheless, for humane reasons they are allowed to remain in Japan even though Japan almost never grants asylum to political refugees. This privilege has given rise to the suspicion that persons inside the Japanese government and ruling party not only favor independence for Taiwan, but are also helping young Taiwanese in Japan who are working for independence.

For geographic, as well as historic and commercial reasons, it seems natural for Japan and Taiwan to maintain close ties. Geographically, Taiwan is vulnerable to the caprices of nature. The island is often struck by murderous typhoons which do much damage to the pineapple, cane-sugar, and banana crops that are important exports to Japan and elsewhere. Sometimes, Taiwan is the recipient of disaster relief from Japan, in addition to credits and loans for various industrial projects.

However, because Asia will see what some call "rational readjustments" in the future, Taiwan will doubtless one day buy and sell from mainland China. If so, this may turn out to be a first step in Taiwan-China rapprochement.

But while many Japanese are deeply concerned about what happens to Taiwan, a much larger number appear to be conscious that relations with China proper are of far greater consequence for Japan.

Historically, many Japanese have always admired Chinese art, painting, literature, philosophy, language, and calligraphy. A large part of Japanese culture had its origins in China, although the Japanese have often refashioned the original.

In prewar years, Japanese militarists regarded prostrate China as a younger and delinquent brother in urgent need of big brother's (Japan's) tutelage. The recognition of China's fratricide, corruption, and weakness made many Japanese contemptuous of China. Of course, many Chinese also agonized at conditions in their own country.

For some Japanese intellectuals and liberal politicians the situation has reversed itself. Japan, they say, should now lend an ear to what the new China has to teach. A few years ago, Japanese elder statesman Kenzo Matsumura, now deceased, delivered this stinging remark after returning home from a visit to Peking: "Generally speaking, I felt that the Chinese are adults and that we are children."

By and large, the Japanese people want to establish a warm friendship with the mainland. Opinion polls show this; intellectuals and most large newspapers campaign for it; the major opposition parties, the Socialists and Komeito, are working for rapprochement and occasionally send good-will missions to Peking.

In response, government leaders regularly affirm as a principle of policy the desire to establish normal relations with China. Periodically, when some major event occurs, such as the Nixon visit to China, the Tokyo government, in reaction to it, makes an attempt to improve relations with Peking. But an undertone also is heard, expressed by conservative politicians and businessmen: Japan should act with caution; Japan should open relations with Peking when the time is ripe; Japan should "not rush to catch the bus." It is a rationale for delay, and it works. The status quo is maintained. Trade builds up, but the prospects for diplomatic relations do not seem to get brighter. Perhaps an indication of reality was contained in a statement made a few years ago by Eisaku Sato before he became Prime Minister. He said that Japan and China probably would not establish diplomatic ties during his lifetime. Sato was born in 1902.*

It is not surprising that there is a dim perception among the Japanese people that the wily hand of old-fashioned diplomacy keeps putting up roadblocks to thwart Japan-China friendship.

Does China threaten Japan? The question, seldom asked by the ordinary citizen, has often been raised by government and ruling-party officials, and it has been studied at some length by the Self-Defense Forces. A sampling of government and party opinion during the past half dozen years or so shows the responses are far from uniform:

1965:   (August) "China is peace-loving." —Prime Minister Sato

(November) "The threat to Japan is real, now that China is a nuclear power." —Prime Minister Sato

1966:   "An N-armed China is a menace to Japan." —Raizo Matsuno, Defense Agency Director-General

1968:   "China poses no threat." —Foreign Minister Takeo Miki

1970:   "There is the possibility that once its domestic troubles are overcome, Communist China can have enough military might to attack Japan." —Okinori Kaya, senior ruling party leader

---

* Prospects seemed much brighter after Prime Minister Tanaka took office in July 1972, but the many roadblocks were unlikely to be cleared quickly.

"On Red China's hypothetical nuclear threat—I leave it to God." —Defense Agency Director General Yasu-hiro Nakasone

1971: "No military threat to Japan is impending." —From draft of Defense Agency military build-up plan

Ought Japan to fear a nuclear China, as right-wing critics say? Or is it, as left-wing critics suggest, that nationalism, patriotism, and remilitarization require pretexts such as the presence of a powerful enemy close to Japan, hypothetical or not?

Whether or not China poses a real threat, some Japanese observe that it may be in the nation's best interests for Japan to remain at loggerheads with Peking. This view prevails among various intellectuals and academics who often engage in round-table discussions on "the complex China problem" and seem indulgent toward power politics, which they tend to regard as fixed and immutable.

China's nuclearization has goaded bullish members of the ruling Liberal-Democratic Party and the military establishment into demanding a huge rearmament for Japan, including possession of nuclear arms. One party member, retired General Minoru Genda of the Self-Defense Forces, was identifying China as a nuclear menace even before Peking exploded its first nuclear bomb in 1964. The previous year, Genda observed that the very desire of China to become a nuclear power was itself a threat to the Far East. But it may be that the military habit of being prepared for any emergency causes Japan to pinpoint future threats to the country.

Perhaps a more accurate explanation for the thinking that regards China as anathema is that many hawks in the ruling party bear a grudge against China for having been unbeatable in war, and, afterwards, for having chosen the Communist road to salvation rather than the capitalist.

What would happen if a Chinese nuclear bomb burst over Japan? Peking has said repeatedly it would never be the first to use nuclear arms. But on several occasions the Defense Agency has prepared studies on the probable result of a nuclear attack on Tokyo, presumably from China, since the issue of a Soviet nuclear threat is scarcely raised by Japanese officialdom.

When the scholarly Governor of Tokyo, Dr. Ryokichi Minobe, who was formerly an economics professor, was asked whether he knew the results of surveys made by the Defense Agency on hypothetical bomb attacks on Tokyo (the world's largest metropolis, with nearly 12 million people), Dr. Minobe shook his head.

Here is what the Governor did not know.

A Defense Agency survey in 1964 said that if a 10-megaton H-bomb, which is five hundred times more powerful than the Hiroshima bomb, struck Tokyo, it would kill outright 4 million persons or almost half the city's then population of 9.9 million. In addition, 2.3 million people would suffer serious injuries, and another half million would be slightly injured. The agency was quite specific; it said its calculations were made on the assumption the bomb burst above the heart of Tokyo on a cloudless day with about 20 per cent of the people outdoors at the time. The Agency described the casualty figures as "tentative."

Another study in 1967 was more grim. Describing similar conditions, the Agency said that only 2 million people would survive. The city's population had meanwhile climbed to 11.1 million.

Still more deadly was a war scenario put together by a

team of four well-known Japanese scholars and defense analysts. The scenario was drawn up in 1966 to assess the consequences of a U.S.-China thermonuclear war. The findings were devastating: almost the entire Japanese race would become extinct, leaving behind an uninhabitable land. The bomb attacks in the scenario were mainly directed against the huge military complexes located near Tokyo and Yokohama. Although such a war is not now deemed probable, the military services of both the United States and Japan are making preparations against Chinese missiles.

It takes eight seconds for a missile to travel from China to Japan at their closest points. Obviously, it is hardly enough time for any effective defense. After China became a nuclear power, however, a half-dozen former civilian chiefs of the Defense Agency drew up defense measures to cope with and offset China's nuclear progress, even proposing construction of nuclear bomb shelters in Japan. The proposal wasn't adopted, but it illustrated the thinking of men close to the seat of power.

Japanese military men on active duty are singularly calm about China. They display no fear of an overt Chinese action against Japan. Foreign experts, too, have minimized China's potential for aggression. *The New York Times*'s Hanson W. Baldwin said in 1970 that China had little or no strike capacity outside its borders. He wrote: "China's navy is essentially a coastal defense force with no long-range amphibious capability. . . . China has limited air and naval strength and its forces have virtually no strategic or long-range mobility." Aside from Peking's increased nuclear power, the situation does not appear to have changed markedly.

A long-term study of China from the viewpoint of Japan's future security was begun by the Defense Agency in February 1971. The study commenced at a time when the U.S. Defense Department was also beginning to pinpoint a future Chinese missile threat.

But it became a dilemma for the SDF to name China officially as a country that truly threatens Japan, as seen from the drafting of the defense White Paper of 1970. The mass media reported that the Defense Agency was sorely puzzled over whether a menace from China existed when it drew up the White Paper. In preparing it, the Agency wished to spell out, if possible, the idea of who might actually threaten Japan. But such expressions as "hypothetical enemy" and "target country" were taboo. The public simply isn't persuaded that Japan has any enemies; and, officially, Japan has no enemy, not even a hypothetical one.

Consequently, the Agency had no wish to stir up the Japanese public unnecessarily. Finally, the Agency came up with a kind of semantic solution to the problem. It raised the possibility that "potential disputes" might break out; then it said that China could "significantly influence" such disputes. One didn't need a particularly fertile imagination to figure out who Japan's probable enemy might be.

The real menace, according to Japan's hawks, is ideological. This is a serious problem because the Japanese people are, in the words of the hawks, ideological adolescents. To them, China is an archrival as well as an enemy. General Genda, now retired and a conservative lawmaker, explains that China ought to be feared because Japan and China share the same written language and have much ethnic, cultural, and historical affinity. For reasons such as these, some zaibatsu industrialists also tend to favor the status quo in Tokyo-Peking relations.

Personal contact between the two neighbors is limited, as might be expected. About three thousand Japanese, mostly merchants, visit China each year via Hong Kong, since there are no direct flights between Tokyo and Peking. From the world's most populous country, fewer than one hundred people visit Japan in a year. The Tokyo government discourages travel to China, and although the interest in the Chinese language is growing, it is still small. It is estimated that the ratio of Japanese presently studying Chinese compared to those studying English is about 1:6. But some say the ratio in favor of English may be much greater.

To guard against rising Chinese power, the late Vice President of the ruling party, Bamboku Ohno, suggested in the 1950's the formation of a United States of Japan that would include Taiwan and South Korea, Japan's former possessions. In recent years, senior adviser Okinori Kaya has urged a common defense network consisting of Japan, South Korea, Taiwan, and the Philippines. In reality, this network exists in embryo, since these nations maintain military pacts with the United States and have significant political and economic ties with each other.

Kaya is a representative ruling party hawk on China. He will, he says, approve of Japan's recognition of the Peking regime when China agrees, first, not to foment a Maoist revolution in Japan, and, second, agrees to recognize the Japan-Republic of China (Taiwan) treaty and the U.S.-Japan security treaty. He too believes that, with regard to the evils of Marxism and socialism, the Japanese people are ideological children.

Japan's foreign policy calls for undiminished support and assistance for Taiwan. This is natural and proper, say Japanese leaders, because Japan owes a debt of gratitude to Generalissimo Chiang Kai-shek's regime for agreeing to waive war indemnities against Japan. They also say that Chiang gave very charitable treatment to Japanese repatriates at the war's end.

In the eyes of the Chinese on the mainland, Japan is guilty of ingratitude to Peking. In 1967, the then Foreign Minister Chen Yi told a group of Japanese visiting in Peking that Mao Tse-tung was very lenient to the Japanese. He said: "Did we kill even a single Japanese prisoner of war? No. We released thousands of Japanese war criminals without executing even one of them. It was possible for us to pass judgment and execute them, but we did not venture that." Also: "We firmly maintained this conviction even when the Japanese militarists invaded our country. This fact will be well understood if you read the books Chairman Mao wrote at that time."

It is estimated that 10 million Chinese were killed and injured during the long Sino-Japanese War (1931–45) and that the total damage and theft of Chinese property totaled $50 billion. So it was a tidy saving for Japan to have diplomatically chosen Taipei over Peking in 1952. The record shows that U.S. officials elicited from Japan a promise to recognize Taipei—and not Peking—in exchange for having the U.S. Senate ratify the peace treaty with Japan.

The cruelty of Japanese troops in China is not well known even today by many Japanese. For example, a group of Japanese social critics, including the late Soichi Oya, traveled to Nanking in 1966 during the height of the Cultural Revolution and asked to see the museum showing pictures of the ghastly past. Seeing photographs of the Rape of Nanking, Oya said: "Yes, it's true; I was there as a reporter." And he related the incident of two drunken soldiers who bet each other who could finish off one hundred Chinese first; how each set out and dispatched with a sword every man, woman, and child in sight; and when they reached about eighty, the soldiers lost count and started the killing all over. The Japan Year Book, 1946–48, mentions the "appalling reign of terror" in which twenty thousand men, women, and children died. It states: "For four weeks the streets of Nanking were splattered with blood and littered with mutilated bodies, while Japanese soldiers ran amok, causing untold suffering among the civil population."

The Peking regime, however, has made it reasonably clear that China would not demand reparations from Japan, saying that China would "not build socialism with reparations taken from the Japanese people." Aiichiro Fujiyama, after a visit to China in 1971, confirmed this Chinese position.

This Chinese attitude of not demanding reparations is, of course, designed to win the friendship of the Japanese people. But the Chinese people, whatever their ideology, have always been known to be patient and slow to anger. Japanese playwright Junji Kinoshita relates how the Chinese had a custom that when they were struck by others and had their teeth broken, they would not spit out the broken pieces but would gulp them down in silence. Of course, this may apply only indirectly to today's Chinese who have "stood up" under Mao Tse-tung. But it emphasizes the cruelty and injustice that the Chinese suffered for ages at the hands of foreigners as well as from their own people.

China believes that it is Japan which is perpetuating hostility between the two countries. Not surprisingly, the

Chinese have encouraged all efforts from the Japanese side to improve relations.

To resurrect Japan-China friendship, various proposals have been advanced by the Socialist Party, by Komeito, and others. Also, a nonpartisan parliamentary body in favor of restoring Japan-China diplomatic relations has been formed with Aiichiro Fujiyama as chairman. However, although it contains a majority of the Japanese Diet, this group appears unable to cause a shift in Tokyo's basic China policy.

Takeo Miki, a conservative lawmaker and former Foreign Minister, and a graduate of the University of Southern California, has suggested four ways to remove friction in the Far East. Japan, he said, should (1) try to know more about China, (2) ease China's excessive wariness of Japan, (3) correct mistakes in China's analysis of world affairs, and (4) correct mistakes in judgment about China among other non-Communist nations. It is a tall order, though doubtless a good one.

Zentaro Kosaka, another ruling-party leader who is also a former Foreign Minister, suggested in 1970 that Japan issue a "no-war" declaration with regard to China as a first step in erasing tensions between the two nations. Speaking in the Diet, Kosaka said Japan should agree never to fight against China, even to the remotest generations. But, Kosaka recalls with regret, the suggestion was turned down by the Cabinet, which said the peace Constitution was sufficient to that end.

Aiichiro Fujiyama once remarked that he thinks too few Japanese have reflected on the war against China. He said: ". . . China still recalls vividly the aggression by Japan and it harbors strong uneasiness that our nation may start the same kind of aggression again." His conclusion: "If we look at the facts of the past, we can understand China's thinking very well."

But, as previously noted, ideology poses a big hindrance to friendly ties. The following incident is not unusual. China has long wanted to sell meat to Japan. This desire has been blocked by lawmakers who raised the issue of sanitation and pre-inspection of the meat. Other lawmakers complained that cheap Chinese meat would hurt the business of their constituents in the meat industry. But this factor wasn't true at all, reported the *Yomiuri Shimbun*, a nationally circulated newspaper, which judged that the opposition grew out of "pure hatred of China."

Recognizing the existence of passionate feelings against China, Kaheita Okazaki, an ex-banker and industrialist who now helps arrange the periodic Japan-China trade talks, has offered his own recipe for detente: "The place disliked by us should be studied harder."

There was, for some time, the widely held impression that the United States was exerting great pressure on Japan not to increase trade and other contacts with China. In addition, it may have seemed for years that Washington's China policy was the most inflexible of any nation. At one time, in the 1960's, a former Japanese Ambassador to Britain, Haruhiko Nishi, wryly suggested that Japan send a "peace corps" to Washington to help soften American attitudes toward Peking.

In 1965, Marshall Green, one of the U.S. State Department's ablest diplomats, in a single policy speech on China, called the Chinese "xenophobic," "sinocentric," "impervious to foreign ideas," "menacing," "expansionist," and "singularly fierce and inflexible." Green, a specialist on Asia, also referred to Mao Tse-tung, saying that "no dictators brook criticism." A year later, China was in the thick of its Cultural Revolution, probably the most sweeping demonstration of self-criticism ever carried out by one nation.

Six years later, President Nixon traveled to China (Green was a member of the Presidential retinue). Because the U.S. government had not consulted with Japan beforehand, the Japanese were understandably irritated; they also felt isolated, a Japanese feeling which many experts on Asia have increasingly worried about. After Nixon's trip, Taiwan was less certain than ever about what the future might hold. Nevertheless, some observers were saying that, as a result of the meeting, America's China policy appeared to be more coherent and adjustable than Tokyo's.

10

America: Ally or Watchdog?

U.S. policy towards Japan, since the Occupation ended and the Korean fighting stopped, has been a clumsy mixture of cultural flattery, pious expressions of friendship, and a series of economic and political pin-pricks.

> —Martin Bronfenbrenner, U.S. economist, from his article for *Mainichi Daily News*, 1964

I find one thing in common between Japan prior to and during the war and present-day America: an attempt to force their peculiar ways of thinking upon other peoples.

> —Soichi Oya, Japanese critic (1900–70). Remark made in 1967

It took two decades for the United States to admit what others had been saying for years: that the postwar conversion of Japan from dictatorship to democracy might be spoiled by a new wave of nationalism with militaristic overtones.

But, at the same time, there was the suspicion that the United States officially looked upon a Japanese swing further to the right as a step toward bolstering the military alliance between both nations. This suspicion was nourished by the fact that Washington's best friends in Japan include right-wing politicians, and businessmen, many of whom do not conceal their preference for authoritarianism.

Nevertheless, there has been a growing concern by Americans about the way Japan seems to be drifting. For example, there were pertinent remarks about dangerous prospects for Japan contained in a 1970 study report of the Foreign Affairs Committee of the U.S. House of Representatives:

The study mission evidences concern over Japan's emphasis on the new militarism. . . . There seems to be a readiness to commit a substantial portion of Japan's vast wealth to the re-establishment of a major international military force. This involves increased spending and much broader definition of its area of defense, nuclear capabilities and a clear determination to be a military power on a scale not contemplated since World War II.

Shortly before this unusual report was released, the danger of new militarism in Japan was raised by a member of this study mission, Representative Lester L. Wolff, in an interview in Manila. Wolff said the budget for Japan's defense forces was doubling every five years, and "that goes on in geometric proportions."

Professor Reischauer, a former Ambassador to Japan, has also noted the increased tempo of Japanese military spending and has pointed out that a shift from 1 per cent to merely 2 per cent of the gross national product for military purposes would make Japan, in short shrift, the greatest naval and air power in Asia.

Given the past performances of the politicians and the military, the rising apprehensions ought not to be dismissed out of hand.

Wolff, a congressional expert on Asia, also said: "I have a good memory which precludes my thinking of Japan as a military power again. . . . I don't think the Philippines has that short a memory either. . . ." * He said he was also concerned about an emerging military-industrial complex in Japan.

The Nixon Administration, too, raised the possibility of resurgent militarism in Japan. High Nixon Administration officials were quoted by the press in August 1970 as saying Japan could become a militaristic nation if the Japanese thought America planned to withdraw from Asia. An alternative, said the sources, was that Japan might join the Communist states if it became convinced Communism was going to dominate the entire region.

---

* It is estimated that 1 million Filipinos out of approximately 16 million lost their lives as a result of the war with Japan. The Filipino economy was shattered, and Manila was pronounced one of the world's most devastated capitals.

It appeared to be the first time that any high U.S. officials had commented so forthrightly on Japan's future and recognized some ominous possibilities.

Meanwhile, a close adviser to President Nixon, who was thought to be Presidential adviser Dr. Henry Kissinger, was quoted in the press as saying that if the militarists returned to power in Japan, such an event would be due entirely to "internal Japanese circumstances."

Such remarks may have been an Administration tactic to scare Congress into keeping U.S. military forces in Japan and elsewhere in the Far East. But the significance of these comments probably goes deeper. It could also have been a simple admission from Washington that circumstances exist in Japan that could force a militaristic revival.

The State Department, meantime, produced a rather novel reason for stationing U.S. military forces in Japan. U. Alexis Johnson, the Undersecretary of State for Political Affairs, told the Senate that American bases in Japan were a watchdog over Japan's Self-Defense Forces as well as a guarantee of Washington's pledges to its Asian allies, such as South Korea. These bases, said Johnson, helped inhibit the Japanese from securing nuclear weapons. Presumably he was referring to the hawks. This prevention, he said, made up a major element in American policy toward Japan.

But if the Senators accepted the explanations, it seemed the Japanese did not. Despite U.S. assurances of military protection, Japan was steadfastly refusing to ratify the treaty banning the spread of nuclear arms.

U. Alexis Johnson gave additional testimony that lent support to the idea of the U.S. watchdog role in Japan. He said America had no air or ground forces in Japan for the purpose of defending Japan against an invasion with conventional weapons. "This," said Johnson, "is now entirely a Japanese responsibility."

Was it possible this official American concern over Japan's political future revealed a modicum of remorse for having pushed Japan in the direction of wholesale rearmament? Be that as it may, Washington has never slackened its pressure on Japan for military build-up, and only a few experts have either questioned this policy or spoken out publicly about some of its disadvantages.

The perplexity is seen in a 1969 editorial of *The New York Times*. On the one hand, it asks Japan to increase its military defenses; on the other, it warns that Japan "must resist a potential militarist revival."

Not only has America encouraged Japanese rearmament, it has also been urging Japan to expand its role in the defense of Asia and the Pacific. Moreover, U.S. and Japanese military forces have sometimes pooled their resources to draw up hypothetical war studies, such as Three Arrows and Operation Bull Run. The plans detail Japanese and American responses in Korea in case of a second Korean War.

According to the Americans, Japan has been elevated into an equivalent NATO partner, making it as vital, strategically, to Washington's Asia policy as West Germany is to the defense of Western Europe.

In 1971 the U.S. Secretary of Defense, Melvin R. Laird, said America was "going to establish a rapport with Japan much as we have done with the North Atlantic Treaty Organization leaders." The meaning for collective security in the Far East seemed clear: Japan's military would be built up more rapidly in order to strengthen the position of Japan as the nerve center of anti-Communist Asian security between South Korea and Taiwan.

Some proof of this role was seen in the completion of a secret underwater communications cable between Okinawa and Taiwan in 1971. Moreover, we have seen the Japanese government's strong interest in a continued anti-Communist regime on Taiwan.

A group of South Korean National Assemblymen charged in the mid-1960's that documents had been secretly compiled spelling out Japan-South Korean military obligations, as requested by Washington. Since mystery and humbug have been the rule in Far Eastern politics for decades, it is difficult to assess the genuineness of the charges.

But although they were never officially admitted, they seemed marginally believable. Japan and South Korea were asked to provide bases for American nuclear submarines, and Japan's defense industry was assigned the task of producing weapons and other munitions for the use of South Korean military forces.

Various dangers attached to making Japan a complete NATO ally were pointed out some years ago by British historian Arnold J. Toynbee. He urged Japan to look closely at what had happened to West Germany because of the American success in persuading Bonn to rearm heavily and become an active NATO partner. According to Toynbee, this presumed success of Washington made the prospect of reuniting East and West Germany very dim. Also, the Russians, who have vivid memories of Nazi military invasion and occupation of their territory, were harsh and unyielding for many years in their dealings with West Germany.

Some parallels for Asia are apparent. Japan's rearma-

ment has evoked memories throughout Asia, especially in
China, of Japanese iniquity. Japan still has no peace treaty
with Peking. China is a nuclear power, and Japan is building up conventional military power and has nuclear ambitions. The fact is that while tensions in Europe have
lessened in recent years, those in Asia have not, and if
unchecked they could produce a most unfortunate situation for Asia and the world.

In its so-called NATO status, Japan has shown great
zeal to become a military power in the Far East, as demonstrated by its impressive five-year defense plans. Only the
nuclear powers and West Germany now possess over-all
military superiority to Japan. In addition, Japan has re-
sumed sovereignty over Okinawa, an island bristling with
military bases. In fact, there are so many that instead of
the bases existing among the population, the population
exists among the bases. Or, as a Japanese visitor to Okinawa put it cryptically: "It is not that the bases are in
Okinawa but that Okinawa is within the bases."

A fact often overlooked is that just as soon as the United
States reduces the number of its military bases in Japan—
about one hundred in mainland Japan in 1972—and va-
cates some of them, the Self-Defense Forces usually move
in. As a result, Japan takes over some of the best-equipped
bases in the world, bases worthy of a superpower. The SDF
naturally wishes to overcome the military gap with America.

Sometimes the Defense Agency asks the United States
to postpone giving back a particular base because the SDF
is not yet ready to take it over. The United States usually
obliges. And those citizens who hoped the returned bases
would be demilitarized and turned into public parks or
recreation centers have been disappointed.

A storm of protest arose on March 8, 1972, when, under cover of darkness, a token unit of the Self-Defense Forces occupied a military base in suburban Tokyo which the U.S. Air Force had vacated three years before. Citizens had wanted a housing development built on the site, and this caused the delay in the SDF take-over of the base. Angry demonstrators and newspaper editorials accused the troops of "sneaking" into the facility, and protesters picketed the base.

Those who question the wisdom of America's encouraging the Japanese to rearm have included one or two high-ranking U.S. military men. For instance, Rear Admiral T. T. Shepard, Jr., who was director of East Asia and Pacific Region Affairs of the U.S. Defense Department, has warned against building up a big Japanese war machine. Japanese national interests, he said, may not always coincide with America's. Shepard's position can also be read as a covert argument for maintaining a big U.S. force in the Far East. But there is the implied fear of the consequences of a runaway Japanese military build-up.

Of course, those within the Pentagon who have been critical of U.S. policy toward Japan have been few, and they seem unable to influence the direction of this policy.

Other American experts on Asia, including many former State Department officials, have raised nagging questions about Japanese rearmament and, incidentally, about Japan's future. In a 1971 interview, William J. Sebald, a former Ambassador to Japan, said that while he felt Japan requires armed forces for its defense, the real problem was where to draw the line. Sebald said there were many informed Americans who were afraid that militarism might revive in Japan.

Sebald and C. Nelson Spinks, another former State Department official, were coauthors of a book in 1967 (*Japan: Prospects, Options and Opportunities*) in which they say that certain Japanese traits, such as excessive stress on loyalty and valor, lead to militarism.

"In recent years," they say, "the revival of motion pictures extolling the virtues of the warrior leaves no doubt that even the psychological impact of defeat and a foreign military occupation have not significantly altered this aspect of the Japanese character."

Another former U.S. Government official, Robert W. Barnett, who was Deputy Assistant Secretary of State, showed anxiety when he remarked in 1971 that Japan could have a bright future, but on the condition it rejected militarization.

George W. Ball, a statesman, financier, and former Undersecretary of State, told a House Foreign Affairs Subcommittee in November 1971 that America should not encourage Japanese militarization. "Nothing," he said, "could be more disturbing to the tranquillity of Asia than for Japan to remilitarize." Ball said that instead of asking Japan for a greater military contribution, the United States should make it clear it intends to continue to provide a nuclear umbrella in addition to conventional military bases which add to a feeling of security for Japan. And he said it would "be folly for us to start Japan down that road [toward militarization] by the slightest suggestion or pressure."

Perhaps Ball meant that Washington had already given enough suggestions and applied pressure enough on Japan to rearm and should ease off now because danger signals were becoming visible.

Through such warnings, suggestions, and pieces of information, one gains the impression that many diplomats, scholars, and military men actually believe Japan is at a crossroads, that Japan might make another tragic mistake, and that America must proceed very cautiously and skillfully in its relations with Japan. Some critics charge that America has helped push Japan nearer the edge of the cliff. In an April 3, 1972, column in *Newsweek* magazine, George Ball quotes Defense Secretary Laird as suggesting that Japan might deploy fleet units in the Indian Ocean. Said Ball: "Such pressure is not only self-defeating but dangerous."

Postwar U.S.-Japan relations have been rather smooth, except for some sticky trade problems and occasional political shocks such as President Nixon's China trip, which was a near-disaster for Tokyo's China policy.

One reason is that Japanese officials have been remarkably courteous and obliging toward postwar America, and many are professedly pro-American. Aiichiro Fujiyama, a ruling-party elder statesman, who was Foreign Minister during the 1960 tumult over the U.S.-Japan security-treaty revision, has cynically observed that Japanese tend to be weak toward the strong and strong toward the weak.

When John Foster Dulles was Secretary of State, the Japanese were invariably cooperative and amiable. True, there were monumental problems to be solved, including the peace treaty with Japan and the issue of whether Tokyo should open diplomatic ties with Peking or Taipei. But Dulles does not appear to have encountered major obstacles in dealing with Japan.

The first time Dulles met Shigeru Yoshida, the Japanese Prime Minister, he told his aides: "I have just met a

man from 'Alice in Wonderland.' " Yoshida no doubt
seemed to have come from another age. He frequently
wore cutaway clothes made in London, used a cane, sported
a cigar, and laughed impishly. Invariably, he went along
with U.S. wishes.

Some reports say Yoshida angrily turned down American
appeals for rearmament of Japan in the early 1950's, and
that he even occasionally pounded the table to show his
resolution. But in addressing the National Diet on March
9, 1953, Yoshida said simply that if the United States asked
Japan to rearm, Japan would comply. Being a good diplomat, he added the words, ". . . if it is in the national interests."

It did seem unusual, however, that if "national interests" compelled Japan to rearm, a foreign country would
have to suggest rearmament in the first place. That table
pounding could have been slightly exaggerated. The Japanese public applauds politicians who appear able to stand
up to the Americans.

Anyway, six months later, on September 27, 1953, Yoshida proposed rearmament of Japan for self-defense. He
also urged amendment of the 1947 Constitution which
banned rearmament. Although Yoshida had previously
opposed rearmament, he had in the previous two years
built up a 110,000-man army called the National Safety
Force.

Dulles's imprint on postwar Japanese history goes deep.
It is interesting to note that as far back as the early 1930's,
Dulles was in total agreement with the Japanese claim
that Manchukuo (Manchuria), which was Japanese-con-
trolled, served as an excellent barrier against expansion of
Communism in Asia. Professor Owen Lattimore, the

American Orientologist, says he heard Dulles say this at a luncheon in Peking at that time.*

The following incident reveals the cynicism of Dulles-Yoshida diplomacy when they handled one of the great issues of postwar history: China. In December 1951 Dulles was in Tokyo, and he handed a note to Yoshida, asking him to put it into a letter addressed to him, Dulles.

In the note, Japan was to promise to sign a peace treaty with Generalissimo Chiang Kai-shek's Nationalist Chinese government on Taiwan, and not with Mao Tse-tung's Communist regime in Peking. American senatorial feeling was then severely anti-Peking—the Korean War was on—and Dulles urgently needed written assurance from Japan in order to get quick Senate approval of the Japanese peace treaty, the document that would restore Japan's sovereignty and permit it to be an ally on equal terms with the United States, at least in theory.

It is often said that Dulles forced Japan into recognizing Taiwan rather than mainland China. But concerning the above letter, Yoshida told Dulles: "We'll be glad to give you such a letter. Why don't you write something up and let me see what it looks like." That's how friendly relations were, according to William J. Sebald, who was present at the Dulles-Yoshida meeting.

After Japan's sovereignty was restored, the country vaulted from poverty to prosperity, spurred by the Korean and Indochina war booms. In both wars, Japan was a

---

* Dulles also left his mark on U.S. relations with China. In 1971, Chou En-lai could still recall, to a meeting of Japanese visitors in Peking, how at the Geneva Conference on Indochina in 1954 Dulles approached him holding his coffee cup in his right hand so that, said Chou, he would not have to shake hands. Probably, President Nixon, during his visit to Peking, was acutely aware of this incident. He was very attentive to Chou.

valuable staging area and depot for U.S. operations, in addition to being an indispensable repair shop for ships and planes. Both wars helped put an end to economic slumps in Japan. Between 1950 and 1953, special procurements in Japan by U.S. military forces totaled as much as $2.5 billion. Japan's exports also recorded a sharp rise. Escalation of the Vietnam War in 1965 solved a partial economic slump in Japan due to frantic overexpansion of production facilities. Exports of steel and machinery to the United States rose by about 70 per cent and 50 per cent, respectively, in that year, and other exports also boomed. Not all exports, of course, were directly related to the war, but some of them freed American industry for direct war production.

Referring to the Indochina War, a Japanese businessman in Saigon once boasted that if it were not for Japanese help of one sort or another, the United States war effort would fizzle out in seventy-two hours. No doubt the businessman was including the American use of Japanese bases, Japanese goods sold to American forces, U.S. Navy supply ships manned by Japanese crews, and the repair of U.S. warships and planes in Japan. Japan was playing a considerable though subsidiary role in the war.

Probably, Americans have been guilty of indulging Japan, lavishing praise without balancing it with criticism. Often U.S. leaders have indiscriminately praised Japanese democracy, industry, economy, culture, and especially its rags-to-riches postwar success story. Professor Reischauer, too, has sometimes flattered the Japanese by saying things like: "Japan is truly the great country in Asia." *

---

* Dr. Reischauer gave this useful explanation in a 1971 interview: "What I endeavored most while I was the Ambassador to Japan was to dwarf the United States as much as possible before the Japanese and to magnify Japan as much as possible before the Americans. . . ."

Doubtless, only superlatives can accurately describe the postwar rehabilitation, as well as the depth and vigor of Japanese civilization. But it often seems that Americans in high places treat Japan as an economic and strategic commodity, completely omitting human values, although the same bad habit may obtain in U.S. dealings in Latin America as well.

From time to time, Americans have tried to dissuade the Japanese from showing too much interest in the mainland, sometimes chiding them for their "facile romanticizing" about China or their "euphoria" toward Chinese culture, although it may be natural among allies to feel jealousy over approaches to a third country.

One sector of Japanese society which Americans, especially those at official levels, have found damnable is the mass media.

In the mid-1960's, the American government openly tilted with the Japanese press, accusing it of being pro-Communist and anti-American. But the press also received reprimands from its own government, which was a favorite target of press criticism.

On rare occasions, the Japanese press could be useful. In 1960, during the huge anti-government demonstrations in Japan, when it appeared to some observers that Japan was on the eve of revolution, the U.S. Ambassador to Japan, Douglas MacArthur II, invited Japanese editors to the Embassy and pleaded for cooperation. After this, the mass media appeared to make efforts to mold public opinion into a favorable reaction to President Eisenhower's scheduled trip to Japan. According to informed sources,* even letters to the editor were carefully chosen in the major newspapers to give the impression that the public

---

* Including Professor Chitoshi Yanaga of Yale University.

was warmly disposed to the Eisenhower visit. This, of course, was not true.

Then, in the mid-1960's, the great issue was Vietnam. The U.S. government was disappointed and sulky, because the Japanese public was inhospitable to the U.S. view of the war.

In 1965, the State Department's specialist on the Far East, Assistant Secretary William Bundy, said that large segments of Japanese opinion seriously misunderstood the situation in both China and Vietnam. Professor, then Ambassador, Reischauer nodded his approval, saying the Japanese government was "perhaps better informed, and that is why it is more understanding than the public." As a careful scholar, he often inserted such words as "seems" and "perhaps" in his political remarks. Unlike some career diplomats, he retained the agreeable habit of fallibility.

A source of distress for Washington was the stream of Japanese journalists crossing Vietcong lines. A few visited Hanoi, from where they wrote vivid and dramatic stories that tended to evoke sympathy for the Vietnamese.

In 1965, the State Department charged that Communists had infiltrated the editorial staffs of *Asahi* and *Mainichi*, whose combined daily circulation tops 10 million. Ambassador Reischauer was appalled at the extravagance of the charges. He issued this statement about the Japanese press: "Even when it disagrees with or criticizes U.S. policy, we admire its professionalism and enterprise, welcome its independence and forthrightness and respect its political integrity."

The *Mainichi* said bitterly: "It must be regarded as regrettable that U.S. policy-makers, with such meager knowledge of Japan, are allowed to continue making Asian policy." The policy-makers, who had made the charges against the newspapers and who had to defend an increasingly vulnerable policy, were a former Ambassador to Japan, Douglas MacArthur II, then an Assistant Secretary of State, and George Ball, then Undersecretary of State.

According to some observers, the result of the American criticism against the newspapers was that the Japanese press moved a shade toward the right. Ironically, although the Americans at the end of the war wished the Japanese press would become one of the freest in the world, many Americans now wished this same press was more pro-Establishment, presumably more like America's.

Then, Japanese newspapers said U.S. pilots were bombing hospitals and schools in North Vietnam, causing civilian casualties. Such reports were filed by two veteran foreign editors, Shoryu Hatta of *Asahi,* and Minoru Omori of *Mainichi.* The United States felt their reports were especially unfriendly. Omori had received two American prizes for excellence in international reporting. He wrote that United States planes had bombed a leper hospital at Kin Lap, in North Vietnam, in daylight for over a week. The attacks took place, he charged, even though the buildings had Red Cross markings and were distant from military targets.

But there was this fact: neither reporter had actually seen the bombings but had watched a film shown in Hanoi. However, Omori and Hatta judged the film to be genuine because of one scene, which showed a legless man who was being carried on someone's back to an air-raid shelter when he was suddenly thrown to the ground by a bomb explosion. "It made us, people from a third nation, want to bury our heads in our hands," Omori wrote on the front pages of the *Mainichi.*

Hatta said diplomats from neutral nations and other

newsmen in Hanoi had convinced him of the film's reliability, although he could not believe that American pilots had deliberately aimed at the leper hospital. Probably, he said, they had misjudged the site or received faulty intelligence. But a few years later, when novelist Mary McCarthy went aboard the nuclear attack carrier *Enterprise* off North Vietnam, she reported that navy pilots said they *never* made mistakes in bombing, thanks to unerring computers and aerial photographs.

On the same day that the editors saw the film report—labeled a canard by the U.S. Embassy in Tokyo—both men traveled outside Hanoi and said they actually saw hospitals and schools destroyed by bombings in other towns far from military installations.

Belatedly, American officials lent their support to the dispatches about Kin Lap. In 1968 the U.S. military spokesman in Saigon, Barry Zorthian, said, prior to his departure from Vietnam: "I wish we in Saigon had made it clearer that our air strikes in the north were not antiseptic, that sometimes [civilian] structures were hit by accident, rather than having the story come as a surprise from correspondents visiting Hanoi." Also lending support were reports of "carpet bombings," as well as the 1971 Pentagon Papers, which included a Central Intelligence Agency estimate that even before 1968 perhaps 80 per cent of the Vietnam casualties were civilian.

Historically, American policy toward Japan has run the gamut of conviviality and hatred, cajolery, generosity, flattery, and fierce competition. As far back as 1921, before he was President, Franklin D. Roosevelt called on Japan to march together with the United States for joint development of Asia's vast resources. The apparent hollowness of the words was shown by America's shortsighted racial exclusionist policies of the 1920's. In 1953, Richard Nixon, as Vice President, visited Japan and appealed for a joint anti-Communist crusade. Such an appeal was balm to the extreme right wing which was eager, then as now, for a fight with American help.

Now it is sometimes said the United States is performing the role of watchdog in Japan. Obviously, the American presence in Japan may inhibit but cannot prevent Japan from going its own way, even if that way leads toward extremism. And, doubtless, adherence to democratic precepts is not a precondition for American friendship.

Nevertheless, the United States could make it repeatedly clear that a militarist course would be intolerable to the American public, and that such a course could only add a persistent chill to the existing tensions between Japan and China and thus hurt the chances for peace in Asia.

II

Moscow and Tokyo

It goes without saying that Japan and the Soviet Union, which are neighbors in the Far East, must place their friendly relations on a lasting basis . . .

—Prime Minister Prince Fumimaro Konoye, 1937–39

Speaking frankly, the Soviet Union is not a country to make friends with.

—Shigeru Yoshida (1878–1967), postwar Prime Minister, who made the remark after he retired from the premiership, in a 1966 interview

The Russian military attaché in Tokyo looked straight into my eyes and said: "Just one of our SS-9 missiles would completely demolish Guam."

Guam, a U.S. territory that is a tropical vacation isle as well as a key air and submarine base, is about 1,500 miles east of the Philippines. It has a land area of 209 square miles, about half the size of Okinawa. That means that only two SS-9's could destroy Okinawa.

One of the most important weapons in the Soviet arsenal, the SS-9 is a liquid propellant intercontinental ballistic missile that can carry a five-ton warhead a distance of ten thousand miles. It is said to be capable of carrying six separate one-megaton warheads, each fifty times more powerful than the bomb used on Hiroshima.

I had referred to Guam because American officials had been quoted as saying that tactical nuclear weapons on Okinawa might be moved to Guam or other smaller islands in the Pacific. When I mentioned the other islands, the Russian said: "For such small islands we don't even need an SS-9."

Actually, there have been many proposals for a nuclear free zone in the Far East, but for one reason or another some of the major countries involved have not considered the proposals worthwhile. And it seems as if the non-nuclear nations must continue to rely on the presumed good sense of the nuclear powers.

Soviet officials have suggested an Asian denuclearized zone combined with a joint security system involving the

United States, the Soviet Union, China, and Japan. Once, in 1967, Victor Maevsky, a Soviet specialist on Japan for the official party newspaper *Pravda,* said that if Japan had no foreign bases and was demilitarized, then the Soviet Union would agree to defend Japan from aggression. It was an interesting idea, but basic and persistent ideological differences have made it virtually impossible for such an idea to be seriously considered.

Nuclear weapons are a delicate subject for the Japanese. Nonetheless, the Soviets have bluntly warned that Japan will suffer disastrously if a major war erupts in Northeast Asia, because of Tokyo's military alliance with America. Such warnings have not endeared the Russians to the Japanese.

On a visit to Japan in 1964, Anastas Mikoyan, then the Soviet First Deputy Premier, said the U.S.S.R. would never point nuclear missiles at Japan, if there were no similar weapons in Japan and Okinawa.

Are there nuclear weapons in Japan? It is a moot question, since U.S. military commanders will neither confirm nor deny reports of such weapons storage.

The Okinawa Council Against Atomic and Hydrogen Bombs announced in 1971 that as many as three thousand nuclear warheads were stored on Okinawa. It was not revealed how such a figure was derived. But it may be noted that in 1966 Robert McNamara, when he was U.S. Secretary of Defense, said there were seven thousand American nuclear warheads in Western Europe.

Without doubt, America does have nuclear stockpiles in Asia. I have seen such weapons in Taiwan. Washington said Okinawa would be nuclear-free after it reverted to Japanese control in 1972. However, diplomatic intrigue and the occult ways of the military make the question of nuclear storage anywhere a matter of lingering controversy.

Russo-Japanese relations are proper and formal, except where the two nations physically converge on the northern seas. There Russo-Japanese relations are frigid. And Japanese military policy adds to the frigidity, for it is drummed into the men of the Self-Defense Forces that Japan must be on guard twenty-four hours a day against "the enemy from the north."

Japanese radar scopes scan the Japan Sea and the northern regions. The radar on Hokkaido, Japan's main northern island, can actually "see" inside Siberia, so that a Soviet plane flying at thirty thousand feet over Vladivostok comes in clearly on Japanese scopes.

At Misawa Air Base, north of Tokyo, maps show these Russian territories and how short the distances are from Misawa: 446 miles to Vladivostok, 375 miles to Sakhalin Island. Russian warships in the Sea of Okhotsk, operating in the Japan Sea, or passing through the channels near the Japanese home islands are monitored and often photographed. Fraternization between the military forces of Japan and the Soviet Union just does not exist.

Except at cocktail parties, there is a minimum of mixing between Russian and Japanese military men, who appear to maintain an enemy complex toward each other.

One day I telephoned the Russian military attaché in Tokyo in order to arrange an interview. He said he was busy on Tuesdays because he was a golf partner of a certain American Air Force colonel who regularly invited him to the U.S. Army's fine eighteen-hole golf course at Camp Zama, near Tokyo. He did not play golf with Japanese officers, he said.

The Russo-Japanese mistrust touches the lives of many thousands of hapless Japanese fishermen who fish in the northern waters, one of the world's richest sources of marine life.

Fishing zones and off-limits areas are carefully marked, but the fisherman's life is filled with many hazards. Japan claims that 10,987 fishermen have been charged by the Russians with illegal entry, and 1,300 fishing boats had been seized up to May 1971, or an average of five ships and forty crew members per month. Sometimes, there are needlessly tragic incidents. On August 9, 1969, for example, the *Fukuju Maru,* a Japanese fishing boat, and a Soviet patrol boat collided. As a result, eleven fishermen lost their lives. The Japanese Foreign Office pointed out that the Russians callously took twenty days to reply to official inquiries about the incident, which further enraged the Japanese public.

The Russians have built military bases on the Kurile Islands, which some Japanese leaders claim to be a threat to Japan. It was only when an American jet plane was forced down by Soviet fighters on Etorup, one of the Kuriles, in 1968 that citizens of Hokkaido first learned the Russians had a major airstrip on the island. Before that incident, the citizens had no idea Russian military bases existed on the northern islands, whose combined area is over six thousand square miles—larger than Northern Ireland or Connecticut.

No Japanese live on the string of Kurile Islands, although the Japanese government claims them as inherent Japanese territory, citing treaties with Czarist Russia of 1855 and 1874. But the Soviets claim the Kurile question was settled by the San Francisco Peace Treaty, in which Japan renounced all title to the islands. However, the Japanese point out that Russia refused to sign the treaty.

In 1956 diplomatic ties between the two nations were

restored, and, in a joint declaration with Tokyo, Moscow agreed to hand back the Habomai Islands and Shikotan Island—they are outside the main Kurile chain—after the conclusion of a peace treaty. A few years later, the Russians reneged, saying they could not return the islands so long as there were American bases in Japan. A few of these islands are so close to Japan's territory of Hokkaido that they may be seen from there with the naked eye.

Even in 1968 Chairman Mao Tse-tung sided with Japan on the Kurile issue, and Chou En-lai once told Japanese guests in Peking he believed the Soviets should return the Habomai Islands as a gesture of friendship toward the Japanese people. Mao first publicly supported Japan on the Kurile question in 1964. In 1965 the Chinese Foreign Ministry said it had been urging Premier Nikita Khrushchev to return the southern Kuriles to Japan.

But the Chinese do not seem to be altruistic only. They have sometimes said publicly that all of Russia's Asian lands were originally grabbed from China.

It is clear that agreement by the Russians to return the northern islands to Japan would open the complex question of other territory which the Russians seized during and after World War II, including Estonia, Latvia, Lithuania, and parts of Finland, Czechoslovakia, Poland, and Rumania.

Yet one may question whether Soviet-Japanese relations will ever become completely normal while the Kurile Islands remain Russian property, and one may also question whether Russia's refusal to discuss the return of the Kuriles is the wisest course. But the Soviet mentality is not hard to understand. In simple terms, the Soviets want near-absolute security for their own territory; they want guarantees that their soil will not again be invaded, or shot at, or blockaded by anyone. If the Japanese controlled the Kuriles, they could blockade Russia's northern exits to the Pacific.

Probably the Russians will not give up these islands unless a pro-Russian government is formed in Tokyo. Another possibility is that the islands will be internationalized at the same time that Japan becomes a leftist or socialist state.

Since the Russians are not about to yield, some impassioned nationalists in Japan talk about recovering the Kuriles by force. But the Soviets seem quite serious about defending the islands. When I was in the Soviet Far Eastern port of Nakhodka, I heard a Soviet sailor say that "anyone who tries to invade the islands will get his face cracked." The Kuriles are, no doubt, well fortified.

Right-wing hatred of the Russians sometimes takes concrete form, and not only in attacks on visiting Soviet officials. One ultranationalist youth group, calling itself the Yasukuni Students League, occasionally holds combat training on a tiny island south of Tokyo for the expressed purpose of warding off an imaginary Russian invasion of Japan. The youths are indoctrinated with the idea that the Soviets may one day launch such an invasion attempt.

This League, incidentally, is demanding revision of the Constitution and state funds for Yasukuni Shrine, where the spirits of the war dead are enshrined. At the 1969 inaugural meeting of the League, the man who delivered the main speech was Minoru Genda.

But it is the Russians who have vivid memories of Japanese soldiers encamped on the Soviet mainland in this century. They grimly remember Japan's invasion of Siberia shortly after the 1917 Bolshevik Revolution and how the Japanese stayed for four years as uninvited guests. An absorbing anecdote tells of an American industrialist who privately asked Lenin to allow large U.S. corporations to develop Siberia and the Soviet Far East. To the surprise of Lenin's colleagues, Lenin agreed. "These lands," he said "are not even in our hands—the Japanese control them." Apparently it was Lenin's idea that if the Americans came into Siberia they would clash with the Japanese occupiers, and this would benefit the Soviet state. But the plan was never carried out.

Of course, there is the view that Russia's return of the Kuriles would dispel some of the Japanese dislike for the Russians. This is the thinking, for example, of steel magnate Shigeo Nagano, who urges Russia to return all the islands. If the Soviets agreed, he says, major breakthroughs would follow in Japanese technical and financial cooperation in Siberian oil and gas development.

The amount of natural resources which remain untapped in Siberia and the Soviet maritime provinces is immense. For example, in the Tyumen oilfields, east of the Urals, an estimated 4 billion tons of low-sulphur oil is available. Moreover, there is said to be enough natural gas in Siberia to supply 10 billion cubic meters of it to Japan each for twenty or thirty years at least. An oil pipeline has already been laid between Tyumen and Irkutsk. A new pipeline is projected between Irkutsk and Nakhodka, on the Japan Sea, for which the Russians desire Japanese financial and technical help.

Besides the territorial problem, a cause of anguish for the Japanese is the periodic haggling over fisheries agreements, particularly crab, salmon, and herring. Although the northern waters are vital to many Japanese fishermen the Russians often lower the fishing quotas drastically and, seemingly, arbitrarily. The Soviets, no doubt, have a valid reason—the need for replenishment of fish resources. But it appears to outsiders that the Soviets often act first and supply the reasons afterward.

In addition to being territorial, the Russo-Japanese problem is ideological and even psychological.

Many Japanese regard the Russians as boorish and stubborn. Few neighbors are more unlike racially, culturally, and linguistically. Nor are they more mutually suspicious. Russians look upon Japanese leaders as two-faced and implacably anti-Communist. In turn, the Japanese think of the Russians as aggressive, as they were during the 1968 invasion of Czechoslovakia.

Even before World War II, a Japanese professor who was describing various nationalities and was obviously anti-Russian, said Russians were physically ugly. Many Japanese view the Soviet nation as a betrayer for having made war on Japan in 1945 although the Soviet-Japanese Nonaggression Treaty was still in force.

Japan was extremely hostile to the Bolshevik Revolution of 1917. Less than a decade later, Japan joined Germany in an anti-Comintern pact. And, between 1932 and 1938, it was reported that Japanese soldiers in Manchuria provoked over five hundred incidents, some of them very bloody ones, on their Siberian and Mongolian borders.

Opinion polls invariably show the U.S.S.R. is one of the least popular countries for the Japanese. A question such as the following is often asked: "With which country should Japan be on the most friendly terms?" The results rarely vary. For example, these were the statistics from a 1971 *Asahi Shimbun* poll:

	per cent
U.S.A.	42
China	21
All nations	6
U.S.S.R.	3
Asian nations	3
Other replies	3
South Korea	1
Non-Asian nations	1
No reply	20
Total:	100

In 1970 *Mainichi,* another respected paper, asked three thousand persons this question: "If you were able to go freely to whatever country you wanted which would you like to visit the most?" The answers:

	per cent
Europe	46
U.S.A.	25
Southeast Asia	14
People's China	5
U.S.S.R.	4
Others and no answer	6
Total:	100

Sometimes the polls ask directly: "Which country do you like the most/least?" Here, too, the U.S.S.R. is always unpopular. But the Russians—as it has sometimes been said of the Americans—do not equate diplomacy with a popularity contest. Moscow, it seems, puts little stock in whether or not it is liked. However, the Soviets have often posted experienced and affable diplomats in Japan, including Nicolai Federenko and Oleg Troyanovosky. The former is an Asian affairs scholar; the latter once served as official interpreter for Nikita Khrushchev.

Japanese nerves are often jangled by the activity of Russian and American warships in the Japan Sea, which was formerly nicknamed the Emperor's Tub because of Japan's tight policing of it. Now, it is more a Russian than a Japanese lake, since it is the indispensable waterway for the Soviet Far Eastern Fleet.

The American Seventh Fleet, too, often enters the Japan Sea, as do Japanese Maritime Self-Defense ships. The United States "showed the flag" there after North Korea's capture of the intelligence ship *Pueblo* in 1968 and the shooting down of the unarmed American EC-121 reconnaissance plane—also by North Korea—in 1969.

In these naval build-ups in the Japan Sea, Soviet and American warships bumped into each other, causing light damage to their hulls. Japanese warships watched discreetly from a distance.

More important, during these crises, it was reported that all Self-Defense Force bases went on full combat alert, demonstrating that what happens to U.S. forces in the Far East directly affects Japan.

The Soviets have two thousand warplanes based in the littoral provinces. They have a hundred submarines in their Far East Fleet, including perhaps twenty-five that are nuclear-powered. All told, they have an estimated six hundred warships in this formidable fleet.

At peak strength, the United States Seventh Fleet had half a million tons of ships, including a number of attack aircraft carriers. The Russians have no such carriers.

Since the Seventh Fleet has its headquarters at Yokosuka Naval Base, near Tokyo, it is not surprising that the Russians sometime send long-range aircraft to snoop over the rim of Japan. These planes, which take care not to enter Japanese air space, have been dubbed the Tokyo Express by Japan's Defense Agency.

Early in 1971, Japanese Supersaber jet planes engaged in mock bombing exercises, swooping down three times to within a few hundred feet of a Soviet destroyer which was cruising in the Tsushima Strait between Japan and South Korea. Japan's Defense Agency said it was an error and apologized.

But the incident may have more significance because each year the Defense Agency compiles a list of foreign ships and aircraft that come close to Japanese territory. The Agency says approximately 4,800 ships pass through the Tsushima Strait each year. And the official Defense White Paper of 1970 showed a chart giving the numbers of unidentified ships and planes which annually appear in the areas and skies around Japan.

Referring to the Tsushima Strait, the White Paper said one or two unidentified destroyers constantly pass through it. So it is of significant interest that the Air Self-Defense Force chose to hold mock bombing exercises in an area where unidentified warships constantly appear.

Although the Russians accepted Japan's apology for the incident, the newspaper of the Soviet Defense Ministry, *Red Star,* called it a provocative act. Japanese planes, it said, often buzzed Russian merchant and naval ships. At least one major Japanese newspaper interpreted the incident as a sign of resurgent militarism.

Despite the sweeping changes in Asia and the world since the Age of Dulles, the so-called Soviet menace remains a cardinal factor in Japanese military tactics. It is not surprising that all Soviet ships in the Japan Sea, and even in the Tartar Strait, which is Russian territory, are tracked by electronic intelligence.

The Defense Agency said in 1971 that it was going to establish about two dozen sets of submarine-detection devices, called hydrophones, on the sea bottoms at the entrance to Soya, Tsugaru, and Tsushima, which are the three major straits around Japan and are also international waterways. This project would be completed by 1976. The cold war in the north is destined to continue for some time.

No doubt was left as to the reason for the plan. The Agency said that in an emergency it was necessary to blockade the three straits against Soviet submarines deployed at Vladivostok and other Soviet Far Eastern ports. Japan, said the Agency, must have command of the seas around Japan in order to defend itself. For this purpose, the Agency also defended the need for combat and patrol planes with the capability of attacking enemy fleets.

The Defense Agency also says it favors a twelve-mile limit on territorial waters, instead of the present three miles. If such a plan went into effect, an anomalous situation would occur: some of the territory claimed by Russia and Japan would overlap in the northern regions.

Actually, both countries have made some headway in other matters, which suggests that much more progress could be made in the future. Japan has set up consulates in Leningrad and Nakhodka; Russia has consulates in Osaka and Sapporo. The first Japanese flights were made over Siberia in 1967. Trade is growing. A five-year trade agreement, ending in 1975, is worth $5.2 billion, an increase of almost $2 billion over the former agreement.

Nevertheless, the Kremlin has consistently and vigorously condemned what it calls the remilitarization of

Japan. The Russians charge that the Japanese right wing is deliberately creating anti-Soviet feelings, especially concerning the northern islands. In Soviet minds, there is a connection between Japan's rearmament and increased calls for the return of the Kurile Islands.

In addition, the Russians appear to be bothered about the renaissance of Japanese revenge tactics. The Soviets, who have a giant military establishment of their own, point out that by the end of the fourth defense build-up in 1976, Japan will have come a long way toward making its military one of the most powerful forces in the world.

12

Politics, Racism, and Nuclear Arms

Japan's gross national product today is such that Japanese businessmen are rapidly taking over markets in a way the generals who preached a Greater East Asia Co-prosperity Sphere never imagined.
> —C. L. Sulzberger, *The New York Times,* March 12, 1972

The resurgence of Fascism and militarism in Japan is a recurring menace.
> —Dr. Ryokichi Minobe, Governor of Tokyo, interview with author, 1971

History will be written by the sword.
> —Attributed to General Charles de Gaulle

The question, "Can there be a Gaullist Japan?" became popular in the mid-1960's when France, led by de Gaulle, disengaged from Washington-dominated diplomacy. The French government recognized China, attempted a pacifying and unifying role in Indochina, and in other ways lent imagination to world politics.

Actually, the Gaullist robes were an ill fit for the Japanese frame. For one thing, Japan is an island nation close to the two Communist giants in the world: China and Russia. Given Japan's anti-Communist stand, its room for diplomatic maneuver would seem to be quite limited.

Further, fierce independence of mind and the wish to break new diplomatic ground are scarcely apparent in Japan. Tokyo's diplomatic mood appears to be governed by precedent, conservatism, conformity, and consensus. Japanese diplomacy also includes a desire, which may or may not be achieved, to harmonize policies as often as possible with America.

There is strong opinion among some observers that if a Gaullist-type Japan did emerge, it would have only a brief life, and would pass quickly into extremism along the lines of prewar and wartime Japanese governments.

Dr. Ryokichi Minobe, the Governor of Tokyo, believes the present mood of the Japanese people, especially their sense of crisis—resulting from anxiety about world economic pressures, tighter economic policies at home, and a feeling of being victimized for being too successful—could even spawn Fascism. A few thoughtful editorial writers, commenting in 1971 on the rise of a neo-Fascist party in Italy, said the same thing could occur in Japan.

General de Gaulle steered his own course partly to halt the American influence in his country and partly to establish his own political and philosophical ideas. Japan's leaders are not nervous about too much American influence. Racial homogeneity and powerful tradition militate against it. But they are deathly afraid of subversion from Japan's Communists and the radical left, whose aim is to bring revolution to Japan.

To block the left wing from inching its way to power, Japan's ruling establishment feels that a new Constitution is needed, one with the prewar stresses on patriotism, discipline, and loyalty. There is the belief that a partial return to some of the prewar controls is both necessary and desirable. The nation is now seeing a further drift to the right.

But now and then the United States is troubled over Japan's desire for autonomy. For example, in a pamphlet issued in 1971 entitled "Military Aid Training in Asia," the Foreign Affairs Committee of the U.S. House of Representatives lamented the trend toward independence inside the Self-Defense Forces.

The pamphlet said the SDF had already gained self-reliance in training as a result of the Nixon Doctrine of self-help. It listed two trends that it deemed unfavorable: (1) the number of SDF men being sent to train in the United States was declining; (2) Japan was heading toward self-sufficiency in armament. Furthermore, the pamphlet cited the Defense Agency's decision to expand its own intelligence unit as another proof that Japan's military dependence on America was drawing to a close.

Shortly after the pamphlet appeared, the Defense

Agency announced plans to establish a $10 million central intelligence office (to be manned initially by a hundred military analysts), as part of the 1972–76 military expansion.

Naturally, the United States expects Japan's military to work as closely as possible with its American counterpart, and there are joint military exercises as well as joint use of certain bases. Moreover, the United States wants Japan to purchase big quantities of American military equipment. However, Tokyo's policy is to expand rapidly its own domestic production of armaments and to make the Self-Defense Forces as autonomous as possible.

But is it a kind of Gaullism? Not when one realizes the Pentagon maintains huge military bases in Japan and Okinawa, including two giant naval bases at Sasebo and Yokosuka, with some of the best ship-repair facilities in the world.

A contemporary Japanese politician who might be considered a quasi-Gaullist is Yasuhiro Nakasone. A patrician of democratic pretensions with a rich political background, Nakasone offers promise for the future as well as reason for concern.

Born in 1918, he has been elected to the National Diet since 1947. He has held important posts in the ruling party and the government, including that of Director-General of the Defense Agency. It was under his tenure as civilian chief of the Agency that the first postwar Defense White Paper was issued, an event of the first importance, because it was, in effect, an attempt to give *de facto* legality to the Self-Defense Forces.

As might be expected, Nakasone is a zealous believer in military build-up. The nation's armed forces are his loyal backers. When he was Director-General of the Defense Agency, he wrote the following lines: "On touring the frontline [sic] and seeing that the young personnel are burning with an unexpectedly strong sense of mission and are serving with great seriousness, I was often deeply moved, and on many occasions, I had a difficult time trying to hide my tears."

Nakasone is suave, articulate, fluent in English, politically adroit, and filled with ambition. During the war he was a naval officer, mostly on land duty. He is one of the most cunning politicians in Japan. He is a hard man to pin down. He socializes with leftist politicians, although he chooses to speak to foreign rather than domestic Communists. He is not anti-Soviet, although he has branded the Soviet Union "treacherous" and "dreadful." He says he is against nuclear weapons for Japan. (He once said: "On the subject of nuclear arms I am not a Gaullist.") Yet he is a firm opponent of Japan's ratification of the Nuclear Nonproliferation Treaty, which would help ensure Japan's non-nuclearization.

He admits to being pro-American, and he is. Of course, friendship with America serves the best interests of Japan's ruling conservative party. However, Americans really do like him. Once, during a speech in California to an audience of winegrowers, he mixed up his lines. He excused himself, saying: "Pardon me, but I'm a little drunk on your wine." Everyone roared with approval.

On the other hand, there is this item: he once was typed as the Hitler of Japan because of his intimacy with the extreme right and also for his perfervid anti-Communism and outspoken remarks on power politics.

Nakasone once ran a private school which seemed more like a small private army—similar to Yukio Mishima's

Society of Shields—than a conventional school. Reportedly, Nakasone's school had eight hundred young men enrolled who were indoctrinated with anti-Communism and patriotism. Their motto was: "Let us sacrifice ourselves for the Showa Restoration!" This appeal for a restoration of the former Emperor system is a theme of many ultranationalist groups. In prewar days it was considered more valorous not just to live and do good deeds for the Emperor but even to die for the Emperor.

I once asked Nakasone about Mishima's private army. He scoffed at it, saying it reminded him of the Takarazuka Girls' theatrical troupe. At that time, Nakasone was head of the Defense Agency.

But is it Gaullist behavior? Probably not. Such traits would appear to mix well with traditional Japanese nationalistic thinking. Even Nakasone said Japan learned from World War II that it must have a powerful ally. This ally is, of course, America.

There is simply too much at stake for Japan and the United States to drift too far apart. The economic facts of life are of paramount importance. For example, it is forecast that by 1980 Japan-America trade may pass $35 billion, more than triple the present level.

Meanwhile, other nations are becoming guarded over Japan's economic thrust. The expansion of the Japanese economy throughout Asia, "with strings attached," casts a big shadow over the politics and life of many Asian peoples. But some voices in other states, including Australia and Canada, are expressing alarm. They are awakening to the possibility of Japanese economic imperialism.

Some Australian economists have wondered whether

their country might drift, within the next twenty years—or by the turn of the century—into being a satellite of the Japanese superstate. W. L. Hutchinson, president of the Engineering Institute of Canada, said in 1971 that Japan was a greater menace economically than she was militarily in the early 1940's. His reason had to do with the pattern of Japan's trade, whereby Canada and Australia, like underdeveloped states, ship huge quantities of raw materials to Japan and buy back manufactured goods, products that could be made by Canadian and Australian industries.

In 1971, over 95 per cent of Japan's $800 million in exports to Canada were manufactured items: radio and television sets, tape recorders, motorcycles, textiles, snowmobiles, and automobiles. On the other hand, almost 75 per cent of Canada's total exports to Japan in the same year ($792 million) were raw materials: minerals, wood, and wheat.

On top of this, Japan's capacity for economic expansion is immense. Mitsubishi officials have indicated that by 1975 Japan would try to pump about $6.4 billion of its foreign reserves of almost $8 billion into foreign industries.

One of Thailand's top economists, Dr. Amnuay Virawan, who is Secretary-General of the Thai Board of Investment, is anxious about his country's future. He has warned that Japan must not be allowed to control every stage of Thai national production, from the raw materials to the final marketing. However, this seems to be the trend. At the close of 1970, two of Japan's zaibatsu, Mitsubishi Petrochemical and Mitsui Petrochemical, along with other Japanese firms, launched the first Southeast Asia "oil combinat" in Thailand. Moreover, since the late 1960's, Thailand has been suffering from an unfavorable balance of trade with Japan.

It is not surprising that some countries in Southeast Asia think they will be overwhelmed by Japan politically and economically. They are suspicious too, that Japan's economic strength may lead in time to the military expansion of the past.

Such fears may be exaggerated, but certain portents of the future may be seen in the increased intimacy and scope of Japan's relations with Southeast Asia. Indonesia, with its wealth of natural resources, such as copra, oil, and rubber, and its strategic location, is an example of Japan's progressing involvement.

In an apparent effort to bolster Japan's voice in that country, the Defense Agency in 1971 said it would like to train Indonesian military officers in Japan. Some Indonesians, such as General Suharto, the national leader, took their officer training in Japan during the Pacific War. The Indonesians responded with an offer of their own. Shortly after the Defense Agency's informal invitation, the Indonesian government asked Japan if it would like to carry out joint aerial maneuvers inside Indonesia. It was a strange proposal, since the two countries are thousands of miles apart. The Defense Agency, which released the information, said it turned the offer down. But some observers believed that the proposals for officer training and air exercises were trial balloons to test the public's reactions to future joint military activities.

At the same time, the Indonesian government disclosed that Japanese industrialists wished to put the Malacca Strait under international control, a step which would give Japan a voice in controlling the strategic waterway. As previously noted, the hawks in the Self-Defense Forces and the Japanese ruling party are eager to see a naval flotilla flying the Rising Sun on patrol in the Malacca Strait.

Perhaps a preview of the future was provided by William P. Bundy who, following a trip to Southeast Asia, observed in April 1972 that Japanese warships might some day be at anchor in Singapore, the mercantile port and giant naval base which lies near the entrance to the Malacca Strait.

The earlier Japanese militarists believed that to have free access to both Northeast and Southeast Asia it was mandatory to possess naval superiority. It is significant that naval build-up is being given priority by the Defense Agency. Since Japan is an island nation with far-flung markets, this development may be wholly understandable. It is nonetheless true that a big naval build-up raises qualms about the future.

Professor Chitoshi Yanaga, of Yale University, says Japan's business circles were quick to realize that the postwar losses of territory in Korea, China, and Taiwan and the end of U.S. military procurements in Japan after the Korean truce could be balanced by finding new markets, especially in Southeast Asia. Moreover, they saw that reparations payments, agreed on in the 1950's and 1960's, could do triple duty: (1) raise the level of Southeast Asia's economy, (2) create new markets for Japanese goods as well as demands for Japanese investments, and (3) help combat the rise of Communism.

Another careful observer of events in the region, Sir Robert Scott, who was formerly Commissioner General for Britain in Southeast Asia (1955–59), thinks the old Japanese dream of a Greater East-Asia Co-prosperity

Sphere may be accomplished finally by economic expansion.

Sir Robert has remarked: "To the outside observer, Japanese have an astonishing capacity to respond to leadership. It has in the past led to disaster." Writing in the October 1971 issue of *Pacific Community*, Sir Robert, who was also the British Permanent Secretary of Defense (1961–63), says: "Success led in the end to Japan's undoing. Japanese pressure to export roused resentment and led to discrimination against Japan. This in turn provoked a military reaction from Japan which culminated in its defeat." And he adds: "The history of the 1930's and 1940's is worth studying because there may be hazards ahead."

Some of General de Gaulle's genius undoubtedly lay in his giving Frenchmen a new pride in themselves as a world power. The Japanese are once again beginning to show considerable pride in their accomplishments and their potential. The fact that Japan's economy, in spite of world fiscal problems, is on the way to surpassing Russia's and to rivaling America's in the 1980's is proof in Japanese eyes of their own excellence—some even say their superiority.

Here is the opening sentence of an article which appeared a few years ago in the magazine *Jitsugyo no Sekai* (*World of Business*): "One of the best traits of the Japanese is that they are a superior race."

Politician Yasuhiro Nakasone concurs. Although his compatriots believe that Nakasone in no way represents the thinking of a majority of the Japanese people, he does carry weight as an important leader of a faction within the ruling party. Once, in pointing out the excellence of

Japan's economic and industrial brains and the merits of the Japanese Zero fighter plane of World War II, he said: "Japan must truly be a superior nation."

Race prejudice certainly exists in Japan and is sometimes criticized by foreigners as well as Japanese. But it is nothing like the super-racism of the prewar epoch. Barbara W. Tuchman in her book *Stilwell and the American Experience in China, 1911–45,* describes the Japanese in the 1920's as "feeling the pricking in their blood of the master-race sensation." In his travels in Manchuria, Korea, and Japan, General Stilwell noticed this characteristic. This prejudice involves minorities mainly, including the Koreans and Chinese, but especially the Koreans, who constitute the biggest minority in Japan. Because the Japanese people are insular, clannish, and homogeneous, many Koreans and those of mixed blood attempt to hide their ancestry in order to advance in Japanese society. Sometimes it doesn't work.

In September 1971 a young Korean using a Japanese name, who was at the top of his class, was promised a job by one of the zaibatsu firms, but when it was discovered that he was Korean he was not hired. It was not a very exceptional case.

A Japanese critic and columnist for *The Japan Times,* Miss Tsugi Shiraishi, wrote in January 1971: "Naturalized Koreans usually have Japanese names, but as soon as the employers find out about the ancestry of the job applicants, excuses are made to reject the Korean job seekers." She also said that employment at big industrial plants is virtually closed to Koreans not because they are inferior to Japanese in skill but because they were born of Korean parents.

More than 2 million Koreans came to Japan before and

during World War II, many of them as forced labor to work in mines and factories and on farms. About 300,000 were impressed into military service. At the war's end, a large number were repatriated, but many decided to remain because of better living conditions and more opportunities in Japan. Today, about 610,000 Koreans live in Japan. The next biggest minority are the Chinese, numbering about 51,000. Many have known no other home except Japan: approximately 72 per cent of the Koreans and 60 per cent of the Chinese were born in Japan, although they are officially classified as foreigners.*

On the grounds that Koreans might influence Japanese undesirably, some private schools have refused to admit Koreans. Despite physical similarities between Koreans and Japanese, intermarriage is not common. Couples who do marry may face ostracism.

Sometimes the nation is shocked into recognition of its prejudice. This happened in 1968 when a Korean outlaw, Kim Hi Ro, demanded a police apology for the discrimination he had been subjected to during his life in Japan. Kim had been feuding with Japanese gangsters and had killed two in a shoot-out. Before police captured him, he called a press conference to publicize his anger and frustration. Later, social critics discussed the nation's prejudice against Koreans.

A scholar, Professor Takeo Shiokawa, said: "The ability to say what had been smoldering in his [Kim's] heart as a result of strong discrimination and long forbearance was released through the murder of two Japanese." A com-

---

* In December 1971, other principal foreign nationals living in Japan included 19,000 Americans, not counting military men and dependents; 3,000 British; 2,545 Germans; 1,650 Canadians; 1,060 French; 870 Scandanavians; 760 Australians; 930 Filipinos; and 630 Italians.

mentator wrote in *Asahi Shimbun*: "We can understand the vexations in Kim's heart."

In addition to their economic and social problems, Koreans in Japan are caught in the web of politics.

The politics of a divided Korea have permeated the Korean community in Japan, which is roughly divided in its sympathies between the Communist North and the anti-Communist South. Since anti-Communist Japan has diplomatic relations with South Korea, Japan naturally tends to favor those Koreans with allegiance to the South. But there are tangled legal issues of residence and citizenship which may never be entirely solved. These issues are of little interest to the average Japanese, but they cause some distress for the Tokyo government. Despite the absence of relations between Tokyo and Pyongyang, the Red Cross societies of both countries agreed in 1959 on a repatriation plan for those Koreans in Japan desiring to resettle in North Korea. Most Koreans who have lived for several decades or more in Japan have come to look on it as their home and do not wish to leave. However, more than 85,000 former Korean residents in Japan voluntarily accepted transportation to North Korea aboard Soviet passenger ships, although they were told they would not be allowed to return to Japan.

The black man in Japan also faces some prejudice, especially the man of mixed blood with one Negro parent, although what is sometimes interpreted as bias may be mere curiosity or ignorance. In 1971 two American black students returned home from Japan disillusioned and angry at encountering some unpleasant experiences. The students complained that Japanese sometimes would touch their hair. In the public baths which they attended, they heard some Japanese wonder out loud if the water might "turn black."

The following incident occurred a few years ago. Children in a Japanese grade school were exchanging letters with children in an American school. But the Japanese pupils were suddenly ordered to stop writing when it was discovered the American children were all black. At about the same time, a Japanese schoolteacher wrote a letter to a Tokyo newspaper saying that since Western nations practiced race discrimination, the Japanese also had a right to this dubious privilege.

Although children of mixed blood in Japan generally lead a miserable life, a class which is truly downtrodden is the *burakumin,* literally "village people." A much less kindly term, which is not frequently used, is *eta,* a word that has a religious connotation of "unclean." The burakumin are sometimes called Japan's untouchables. Some critics have referred to them as "Japan's Negro problem," but the problem is largely economic and social in origin. Even those who harbor prejudice against them acknowledge that they are of the Japanese race.

During feudal times, these unfortunate people, now totaling more than 1 million, performed what was considered the most menial work: slaughtering animals, burying the dead, making animal glue, and so on. They were forbidden to marry into the upper classes and were required to live in special communities, or ghettos. About a hundred years ago, a decree was issued which in theory emancipated the burakumin; but a good deal of prejudice still exists.

Even now, members of the special, or *buraku,* communities found mostly in western Japan suffer indignities such as discrimination in jobs, housing, and marriage. A large percentage of them are unemployed, and many others have lowly jobs. An insurmountable problem is the document of lineage which a man or woman must show to get a job or to marry. With this document it is easy to tell that someone hails from a special community, or once did. It is thus almost impossible to escape the accident of birth. A select few have become successful in politics and the business world.

Burakumin leaders have been partially successful in getting government funds for better education and housing, but these have been a mere pittance. For example, only about $10 million was appropriated for this purpose in 1970, although there are more than four thousand indigent buraku communities. Meanwhile, a National Committee on Burakumin Liberation was formed in the 1960's to break down the traditional attitudes which have condemned more than 1 million Japanese to live in the special communities.

Sometimes, Asians complain about Japanese prejudice against other Asian countries. But many Japanese also feel frustrated over the favoritism Japan shows to Europe and America. Of course, this attention may be only natural: the Japanese are vastly different both culturally and industrially from much of Asia, and they have admired and borrowed from Western civilization for many years. In his memoirs, the late Prime Minister Shigeru Yoshida could say: "We Japanese are in many respects more European than Asian."

Some Japanese felt their country's deference to Western cultural and technological leadership was symbolically continued by Emperor Hirohito's unprecedented visit to

Europe in 1971. True, the Emperor was making a nostalgic journey to some of the places he had seen many years before as a Crown Prince, but they noted with regret that there was little or no prospect for a similar visit by Hirohito to Asian countries in the near future.

Perhaps the biggest anomaly concerning the problem of race and international relations has to do with Japan's ties with South Africa, which practices apartheid against blacks and segregation toward Asians. The Japanese are the only Asians who have been given special status in South Africa as "honorary whites." This separate treatment is accorded because of Japan's exalted position as a major trading partner of South Africa. However, a businessman in South Africa voiced another possible reason for the granting of special status to the Japanese: Japan had sent a small naval flotilla to South Africa on a goodwill visit in the postwar era and, consequently, South Africa's respect for Japanese power had risen immeasurably. Some Japanese feel shame as such special status—which is not, for instance, granted to Indians or Chinese—and would be glad if the Japanese government openly rejected it. There is little chance of this happening.

However, when it comes to Japan's superior industrial ability, Japanese chests understandably swell with pride.

Some Japanese are now showing a pride in their country as a latent nuclear power. Nor is it really a new pride. In 1969, Japan's Science and Technology Agency said Japan had enough fissionable material on hand to produce ten atomic bombs. This nuclear stockpile was expanding, according to the Agency, and would reach over fifty tons by 1985, enough to build 150 atomic bombs. However, Japan's nuclear fuel stockpile is increasing more rapidly than before, and some observers say that by the middle of the next decade Japan will be able to manufacture ten times that many atomic bombs.

In any case, it was a rather surprising statement by an official agency of a country which is supposed to frown on the possibility of atomic-bomb production.

In 1965, Dr. Glenn Seaborg, who was then Chairman of the U.S. Atomic Energy Commission, visited Japan, and I asked him whether Japan would be able to produce nuclear weapons. His answer was slightly technical but he said Japanese reactors would eventually produce enough fuel for many atomic bombs.

But Dr. Seaborg felt there was no need to worry because Japan was among the first nations to place its reactors under the supervision of the International Atomic Energy Agency (IAEA), which includes on-site inspections. He said: "The Japanese have certainly given all indications they wish to operate their program under this system."

That was 1965. Now, Japan appears displeased with IAEA supervision. At the end of 1970, the Japanese made a strong protest to IAEA, saying its inspections were so unreasonably strict that they were hampering smooth development of the nation's nuclear-power generation. However, the inspectors, including Europeans and Asians, refuted the charges, saying they used only a standard procedure for checking reactors, and this procedure was not more strict with one nation than with another.

There was this unusual note: Japan's nuclear energy circles suddenly said the alleged stiff attitude on the part of IAEA would have a harmful effect on Japan's ratification of the Nuclear Nonproliferation Treaty. The Tokyo government has not budged in its stand of not presenting the treaty to the National Diet for ratification.

Two other points seem noteworthy. Up to 1970, the IAEA had conducted over fifty inspections on Japanese nuclear reactors, and there were few, if any, complaints. However, the vigorous complaints of 1970 were made by two of the nation's most prominent industrialists: Kazutaka Kikawada, president of Tokyo Power Company Ltd., and Tomiichiro Shirasawa, president of the Japan Atomic Power Company Ltd. In other words, the protest had much weight behind it. As noted previously, Kikawada is a big-navy advocate who thinks Japanese warships should patrol the high seas.*

Japan's atomic-energy industry is expanding rapidly. Universities turn out about three hundred nuclear scientists each year, and electric-power firms now operate six nuclear power-generating plants, with ten more expected to function by 1975. In that year, Japan plans to have a nuclear-power-generating capacity of 8.6 million kilowatts, and triple that amount by 1980. This capacity would increase to 60 million kilowatts by 1985, second only to that of the United States.

Although the Tokyo government has promised faithfully not to manufacture nuclear weapons, a subtle change in the nation's nuclear policy was discernible in the 1970 White Paper on defense, which said: "If small-size nuclear weapons are within the scale of real power needed for the minimum necessary limit for self-defense, and if they are such as will not be a threat of aggression toward other nations, it is possible to say that possession thereof is possible in legal theory." It is obvious that the wording was

---

* After 1970 there was a hint of a softening, perhaps even a change in thinking, on the part of Japan's electric power officials, reflecting a need for ratification. But it remained to be seen if they could budge the hawkish views of military men and politicians.

prepared with care. What it means is that a pretext now exists for a change in nuclear policy any time the government feels such a change is necessary.

As Japanese rearmament shows a steady advance, the nuclear build-up by the Chinese also adds to the tensions in Asia. The possibility exists, however unfortunate, that Japan and China could become nuclear rivals. In an attempt to prevent the already prevailing tensions from worsening, a few thoughtful men in both East and West have observed that the optimum plan for peace in the Far East may be an arrangement among all the powers immediately involved.

Filipino statesman Carlos P. Romulo has suggested that an understanding take place among the big powers to provide genuine security and stability for Asia. And American diplomat and scholar George F. Kennan has proposed big-power guarantees for the security of Japan. In addition, U.S. Senate majority leader Mike Mansfield also favors this idea. In a speech at the Johns Hopkins University, Maryland, in November 1971, Mansfield recommended "quadrapartite talks" on the establishment of peace in the Pacific. He said there was a "need for a frank confrontation of the four major nations—Japan, China, the Soviet Union, and the United States—whose power converges in the Western Pacific." As the only non-nuclear power of the four, Japan ought to take the lead in calling for such a Pacific peace conference, Mansfield reasoned. But the Japanese reaction appeared cool; not only did Japanese officials generally withhold comment on the proposal, but most liberal newspapers ignored it.

Yet it may well be that the best safeguard against the sudden eruption of a major international crisis in the Far East lies in a four-power treaty, including nonaggression pacts between Japan, China, the United States, and Russia. In the past, the idea of direct talks among the four powers has been shrugged off as impractical or as being against the best interests of Japan. Yet the desirability of such talks, and perhaps their inevitability, seems more apparent with time.

It is becoming clearer that the longer such talks are put off, the greater the chance Japan will emerge as the sixth nuclear power, a situation many observers view as perilous and as likely to impede an early easing of regional tensions.

Meanwhile, the withdrawal of U.S. military bases from Japan will likely produce consequences of major proportions.

A former American prosecutor at the Far East war-crimes trials, Frank H. Scolinos, who practices law in Tokyo, believes that after U.S. forces are withdrawn from Japan (some experts predict this will occur as early as 1975–76), he fully expects an internal upheaval to follow with the military in a pivotal role. He offered two main reasons for his appraisal, which is being increasingly accepted by the foreign community in Japan. First, many Japanese conservatives feel the only possibility of halting the steady growth of Communists and the left wing is to impose controls: more stringent laws against subversion, and, at the same time, reinforcement of the police. In short, a partial return to the regimentation and surveillance of prewar days. Second, there is the belief among many right-wing politicians and military leaders that the two giant nuclear-armed Communist neighbors, China and Russia, are Japan's natural enemies against whom Japan is insufficiently guarded.

Lending powerful endorsement to this prediction is this forthright statement by Japanese Prime Minister Eisaku

Sato, which was made in an interview printed in the September 20, 1971, issue of *Newsweek* magazine: "We still maintain the Japanese-American Security Treaty, which prevents the feared revival of Japan's militarism." Many observers believe that without the existence of U.S. bases in Japan the treaty would be ineffective and unreliable.

However, Japanese suspicions and reservations about the value of the security treaty with the United States are steadily rising. There is the belief that the momentum to a nuclear stance by Japan has already begun.

Appendix

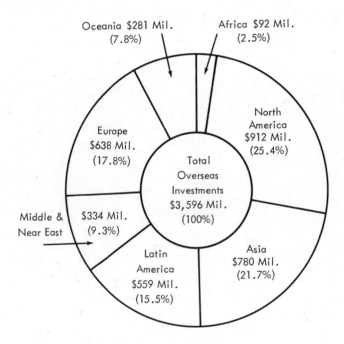

Source: Ministry of International
Trade and Industry

AREA PATTERN OF JAPAN'S DIRECT INVESTMENTS OVERSEAS AS OF
MID-1971

1. In Asia, the principal recipients of Japanese capital were Indonesia, Thailand, the Philippines, and Malaysia.

2. The total of Japan's direct investments abroad at the end of March 1971 amounted to $3.59 billion.

3. The Ministry of International Trade and Industry estimates that Japan's direct investments abroad will reach $11.5 billion at the end of 1975 and rise to $26 billion at the end of 1980. A noted European economist, Hakan Hedberg, has predicted Japan will have made direct overseas investments of $100 billion between 1969 and 1980, a sum that would be four times as large as America's direct overseas investments in the decade up to 1967.

JAPAN'S FLOURISHING TRADE WITH SOUTH AND EAST ASIA, 1971, IN U.S. DOLLARS (1970 FIGURES IN PARENTHESES)

	Exports		Imports	
Burma	58,612,000	(38,722,000)	17,461,000	(12,569,000)
Cambodia	11,836,000	(10,784,000)	2,234,000	(5,991,000)
Ceylon	34,528,000	(24,931,000)	19,060,000	(17,372,000)
China	578,188,000	(568,878,000)	323,172,000	(253,818,000)
Hong Kong	787,372,000	(700,286,000)	98,032,000	(91,803,000)
India	203,883,000	(103,118,000)	376,558,000	(390,061,000)
Indonesia	452,836,000	(315,780,000)	854,466,000	(636,553,000)
Laos	6,220,000	(6,677,000)	25,000	(49,000)
Federation of Malaysia	204,022,000	(166,464,000)	372,566,000	(418,895,000)
Pakistan	113,388,000	(138,428,000)	58,068,000	(42,350,000)
Philippines	464,787,000	(453,717,000)	513,812,000	(533,465,000)
Singapore	507,988,000	(423,034,000)	113,893,000	(86,539,000)
South Korea	855,687,000	(818,175,000)	274,421,000	(228,970,000)
South Vietnam	149,370,000	(146,073,000)	4,190,000	(4,554,000)
Taiwan	923,332,000	(700,418,000)	286,017,000	(250,765,000)
Thailand	445,091,000	(449,195,000)	229,878,000	(189,598,000)

JAPAN'S TRADE WITH SELECTED OTHER NATIONS

	Exports		Imports	
Australia	718,827,000	(589,038,000)	1,752,374,000	(1,507,696,000)
Canada	876,209,000	(563,266,000)	1,004,338,000	(928,589,000)
W. Germany	658,191,000	(550,151,000)	606,874,000	(616,991,000)
U.K.	574,325,000	(479,870,000)	417,126,000	(395,172,000)
U.S.A.	7,495,250,000	(5,939,819,000)	4,977,882,000	(5,559,579,000)
U.S.S.R.	377,267,000	(340,932,000)	495,880,000	(481,038,000)

Source: Japanese Ministry of Finance

A List of Further Readings

Brzezinski, Zbigniew, *The Fragile Blossom: Crisis and Change in Japan*. New York, Harper & Row, 1972. A concise analysis of current Japanese problems with some provocative recommendations such as formation of a "Pacific maritime triangle" between Japan, Australia, and Indonesia.

Butow, Robert J., *Japan's Decision to Surrender*. Stanford, 1954. First-rate scholarship on a very painful episode in Japanese history.

Emmerson, John K., *The Japanese Dilemma: Arms, Yen and Power*. New York, Dunellen Publishing Co., 1972. Provides a needed perspective to many of the issues and events in Japan today. The author is a former career diplomat who served in Tokyo and now pursues academic interests.

Keene, Donald, *Modern Japanese Literature: An Anthology*. New York, Grove Press, 1956. Includes stories by such well-known authors as Tanizaki, Dazai, Kawabata, Akutagawa, Nagai, and Mishima.

Kodama, Yoshio, *I Was Defeated*. Tokyo, R. Booth & T. Fukuda, 1951. The autobiography of a leading ultranationalist.

Mishima, Yukio, *Death in Midsummer*. London, Secker & Warburg, 1967. Includes story, "Patriotism," about a young soldier's suicide with his wife.

Morris, Ivan, *Nationalism and the Rightwing in Japan*. London, Oxford University Press, 1960. An indispensable and exhaustive work on this subject.

Reischauer, Edwin O., *Japan: The Story of a Nation*. New York, Alfred A. Knopf, 1970. A comprehensive and valuable history that also contains good bibliography.

Sansom, G. B., *Japan, A Short Cultural History*. New York, Appleton Century Crofts, 1962. Has lively descriptions of many historical events that helped shape Japanese tradition.

Scalapino, Robert A., *Democracy and the Party Movement in Prewar Japan*. Berkeley, University of California Press, 1953. Excellent for Meiji period politics and some years after.

Storry, Richard, *A History of Modern Japan*. London, Cassell, 1962. A splendid basic history with good bibliography.

—— *The Double Patriots*. London, Chatto & Windus, 1957. Must reading for understanding of ultranationalist movements in twentieth-century Japan.

Wildes, Harry Emerson, *Typhoon in Tokyo*. New York, Macmillan, 1954. Dated but good description of the Occupation.

Wilson, George M., *Radical Nationalist in Japan: Kita Ikki, 1883–1937*. Cambridge, Mass., Harvard University Press, 1969. A scholarly critique of an important ultranationalist.

Yanaga, Chitoshi, *Big Business in Japanese Politics*. New Haven, Yale University Press, 1968. Essential reading for anyone interested in the vital role which economics plays in Japanese political life.

Yoshida, Shigeru, *Yoshida Memoirs*. Boston, Houghton Mifflin Co., 1962. A rather revealing account of the Occupation by the man who was Prime Minister during many of its most important years, and several years after.

Index

Albert Axelbank went to Japan in 1959 after doing graduate work in history at the University of Wisconsin and reporting for local newspapers in Alabama, Virginia, and Ohio. For two years, he was Taiwan Bureau Manager for UPI. He taught briefly at Tokyo's Sophia University. His articles have appeared in *Harper's Magazine, The* (London) *Economist, The* (Manchester) *Guardian, The Nation, The Progressive, The New Republic, Far Eastern Economic Review, The New York Times, The* (Montreal) *Star,* Toronto *Star, San Francisco Chronicle,* the *Times* of India, and many leading Japanese journals. He is thirty-six, lives in Tokyo, and is fluent in Japanese. To prepare this book, he interviewed Japanese political, literary, and military leaders. *Black Star Over Japan* will be published in Tokyo by Asahi Shimbun.

DI

A